Amazing Edible
SEEDS

Vicki Edgson and Heather Thomas

Photography by Yuki Sugiura

Amazing Edible
SEEDS

Health-boosting and delicious recipes using
nature's nutritional powerhouse

jacqui
small

First published in 2017 by
Jacqui Small LLP
74–77 White Lion Street
London N1 9PF

Publisher: Jacqui Small
Managing Editor: Emma Heyworth-Dunn
Designer: Maggie Town
Food Stylist: Aya Nishimura
Production: Maeve Healy

ISBN: 978 1 84780 925 4

A catalogue record for this book is
available from the British Library.

2019 2018 2017

10 9 8 7 6 5 4 3 2 1

Printed in China

Quarto is the authority on a wide range
of topics. Quarto educates, entertains
and enriches the lives of our readers –
enthusiasts and lovers of hands-on living.
www.QuartoKnows.com

Contents

Introduction: the seed of life

Seeds have played a central role in culinary traditions for thousands of years, and are now becoming even more popular as more of us look for healthy and sustainable – as well as delicious – alternatives in their diet. Many people are choosing to limit their intake of saturated fats, and considering the benefits of vegetarian and vegan approaches to nourishment.

But if you're reducing the animal-based proteins in your diet, it's important to make sure that you replace them with other proteins, since the healthy growth and development of all the organs in the body depend on them. Seeds, the life force of every plant, flower, herb, fruit, vegetable and wholegrain we eat, are the building blocks of all vegetable protein, and provide these nutrients in abundance. The nutritional potency of many seeds can be maximized and made more accessible to the body if they are 'activated', i.e. if the enzyme activity within the seeds themselves is triggered by soaking or sprouting them before they are used.

In this introductory section there is information on how the different seeds yield the proteins, essential fats and other nutrients that our bodies need, and there's an easy at-a-glance table to summarize this plus information on how to choose, use and prepare all the seeds that are featured in the book. The recipe section illustrates the versatility of seeds and how they can be incorporated into meals, snacks and even baking and desserts in so many delicious ways.

It may surprise you to discover how much tastier and more nutritious carefully sourced or home-grown seeds are than their mass-produced modern counterparts, which have often been selected to suit industrial processes and farming timetables rather than for their flavour or nutritional content. Many seed companies pride themselves in sourcing seed from non-GM (genetically modified) plants, so you can choose to grow organic material for you and your family's health. Growing your own seeds is not only intensely satisfying but it's also a great way of sharing the fun of planting, nurturing and harvesting produce as well as introducing the lifelong benefits of a well-balanced diet to children in a practical way. Many types of seed can be grown in your own home, on the windowsill, or the smallest of patios, allotments or gardens.

Whichever seeds you choose to grow and cook with, we hope you enjoy the process. This book will give you a glimpse of the enormous benefits seeds contribute, not only to your enjoyment of the food you eat but also to the health and well-being of your body and mind.

Ancient wisdom to modern medicine

Most of the seeds we have selected in this book have been developing on the planet for hundreds if not thousands of years. Many have sustained and been instrumental in the survival of generations of peoples, and used as salves, medicines and tonics as well as for nourishment.

Modern pharmaceutical companies compete to offer the kind of remedies which, in many instances, have been associated with particular seeds or plant extracts for centuries: health-giving properties that have been understood and passed on from generation to generation.

Current health problems that affect the developed world – such as diabetes and obesity – are blamed largely on modern-day eating habits and food choices. Profit and convenience have also too often become the drivers in modern farming and food production, prized above taste and genuine nutrition.

In response to such trends, an increasing number of people are turning to more traditional and holistic ways of feeding their bodies and minds. Choosing to eat organic foods is often a part of this response.

Seed as currency

In previous centuries, spices such as cinnamon, cardamom, ginger, pepper and turmeric were carried long distances to be traded, and foods indigenous to one country became familiar to other cultures. From the Amazon came quinoa, linseed and chia seeds, for example; from Egypt, pomegranate, fennel, sesame and coriander seeds; from India and Pakistan, cumin, poppy and mustard seeds; from Morocco, caraway and hemp seeds, and from Russia, buckwheat.

Some seeds were literally considered worth their weight in gold. The word 'carat', the unit of weight/size of a diamond, derives from the word for 'carob'. It is believed that, because the weight of seeds in the carob pod are so uniform, they were used as units of measurement for diamonds and gold.

Small packets of dense nutrition

The nutritional value of some seeds revealed themselves to new cultures in unexpected ways. During long voyages in the Age of Discovery from the fifteenth to eighteenth centuries, skin and bone disorders, such as scurvy and rickets, were endemic in European sailors, owing to the long periods spent at sea without access to fresh food, especially fruit and vegetables. Sailors who resorted to eating some of their cargo of seeds, however, noticed that they became less susceptible to these common afflictions.

Modern research has – through vastly more sophisticated experiment and analysis – determined the exceptionally potent nutritional content of many edible seeds. Most are packed with the full range of B vitamins, which are vital for metabolic function and energy production at a cellular level.

As the global population continues to rise, we need to establish the best way forward in farming and food production. Seeds – sustainable, transportable miniature powerhouses of dense nutrition and potent fuel – would seem to offer an immensely valuable, readily available resource. Since they're utterly delicious, too, surely nothing should be holding us back!

Seedy yoghurt dressing (see page 107)

What are seeds?

Seeds are plant embryos: their fertilized ovules. Think of them as the plant kingdom's equivalent of animal stem cells: miniatures containing all the information that is needed to form and sustain the next generation.

Different plants are designed to disperse seeds in different ways. Some seeds are transported by wind whereas others are designed to float, glide or spin through the air. Plants growing near water may use currents to transport their seeds. Some pods literally explode, scattering their seeds some distance away from the parent plant and in many different directions. Many plants use animals to carry off their seeds, having evolved seeds with 'hooks' that attach to passing traffic. Some seeds are enclosed in colourful or fragrant fruit, which attracts animals and birds to eat them. The undigested seeds are then eventually deposited as waste, to grow perhaps many miles from the parent plant.

Seed groups

From the scores of delicious and nutrition-rich edible seeds we might have chosen, we have identified our top twenty. In the following pages, we set out their powerful health-giving properties, touching also on their historical origins and the different forms in which they are found, before illustrating their delicious versatility in the kitchen.

Seeds bring colour and flavour as well as essential nutrients to an enormous variety of healthy dishes ranging from irresistible snacks, drinks, breakfasts and salads to suppers and desserts.

There are many different ways to categorize seeds, some of which overlap and appear to contradict each other. The confusion stems from the fact that many so-called seeds are, in the botanical sense at least, not seeds at all but fruits, dried fruits or grains. Some, such as sunflower 'seeds', are technically not seeds until their outer shell (pericarp) is removed, and yet commercial sunflower seeds are sold as such whether they are enclosed within the hard wall of the fruit or 'shelled', with the inner edible part exposed.

We have divided our seeds into four simple groups according to their position on the parent plant:

First come **fruits** (pages 12–15): caraway, coriander, hemp and mustard seeds.

Second are seeds that are contained **within the fruit** itself (pages 16–21). Pods are included here, being the fruits of a specific orchid plant. This group comprises alfalfa, cardamom, cumin, fenugreek, nigella, pomegranate and vanilla.

The third group is **flower heads & kernels** (pages 22–25): fennel, poppy, pumpkin and sunflower.

And the fourth is the group known as **pseudocereals** (pages 26–29). These are termed pseudo because the stem on which they are held is not harvested for the grain at the tip, but for the seeds, which are used whole rather than being ground into germ and flour, as with wheat and barley. The group comprises buckwheat, chia, linseed (also known as flaxseed), quinoa and sesame.

Uses & values: fruits

Caraway *Carum carvi*

Sometimes known as 'Persian cumin', caraway is a member of the parsley or Umbelliferae family, which also includes dill, fennel and anise, and is native to Europe and Asia Minor. Like the rest of the family, the 40–60cm (16–24in) tall plant has feathery leaves, and the small creamy white or pink-tinged flowers grow on short stalks in clusters, spreading out like ribs from a central point on the stem.

The pointed 'seeds', which are similar to cumin in appearance, are actually the split halves of tiny, ridged, crescent-shaped fruits. Their name is derived from the ancient Arab word *karawya*, and they were mentioned by the Roman writer Pliny as a seasoning for food and for sprinkling on bread. Caraway seeds appear over the centuries in many works of literature – even Shakespeare writes of Falstaff being offered 'a pippin and a dish of caraways'.

The little seeds are packed with nutritional goodness. They are a rich source of soluble and insoluble dietary fibre and speed up the transit of digested food through the large intestine, thereby preventing constipation. Their fibre binds to toxins in the gut, which not only helps to remove them more effectively but is also thought to protect the lining of the gastrointestinal tract. They are used medicinally by some people to help prevent flatulence, heartburn and bloating and to improve digestion.

Because they have a very low glycemic index (GI), the seeds help to regulate blood-sugar levels, while delivering the vital nutrients our bodies need for energy production. The seeds possess numerous antioxidants (capable of removing potentially harmful oxidizing agents), including beta-carotene, lutein and zeaxanthin which, in research trials, have been found to help lower the risk of intestinal cancers.

They are also an excellent source of many minerals, including iron and copper, that help red blood cell formation, and potassium, which helps to regulate blood pressure and support the cardiovascular system.

Like most seeds, caraway are rich in selenium, an important mineral for maintaining a healthy immune system, along with zinc, which is involved in most enzyme processes in the body, including digesting protein, healing and repairing body tissues, and male fertility.

Calcium, magnesium and manganese are also found in caraway, and they are collectively important for the health of bones, ligaments and tendons. Vitamins A, B-complex, C and E are also present.

Caraway seeds contain essential oils and have a distinctive, slightly bitter taste and a pungent aroma. Their warm and aromatic tones add a peppery fragrance to a variety of dishes, ranging from Hungarian goulash to traditional seed cakes and baked cheesecakes. Their taste works especially well with the brassica family of vegetables (cabbage, cauliflower and broccoli). Add just a teaspoon or two to some lightly steamed or stir-fried cabbage with a little butter or crème fraîche and a grinding of spicy black pepper to elevate this humble vegetable into something special. Caraway seeds have long been popular in Eastern Europe, Germany and Scandinavia, where they are an important ingredient in soups and dark rye bread as well as local cheeses.

Coriander *Coriandrum sativum*

The dried fruit of the coriander (cilantro) plant
– also known as Chinese parsley – are used as
culinary seeds throughout China, India, Mexico,
Latin America, the Middle East and North Africa.
Like caraway, coriander (cilantro) is a member of
the Umbelliferae family of plants. Its name evolved
from the Greek word for a bed bug, *koris*, perhaps
due to the distinctive scent of the flat-leaf-parsley-
shaped leaves. The spicy seeds are available whole
or ground into powder.

Coriander is among the world's oldest spices – it
is even mentioned in the Bible. When some dried
remains of the plant were found in Tutankhamun's
tomb, archaeologists speculated that it was grown
for food in ancient Egypt (it is not native to the
region). It was also used by the ancient Greeks and
Romans as a preservative as well as a flavouring.
Even Hippocrates, widely regarded as the founder
of medicine, recognized its properties and
recommended it as a tonic for blood circulation.

Coriander seeds can make a valuable
contribution to maintaining a healthy immune
system. They contain anti-bacterial and anti-
microbial compounds, which help keep the
digestive tract healthy and fight salmonella, listeria,
e.coli and other food-borne illnesses. They are also
a good source of vitamin K, which is necessary for
clotting blood in the body's healing processes, and
antioxidant carotenoids, including alpha- and beta-
carotene, essential for healthy retinal cells.

The dried seeds have a warm, spicy, citrus
flavour and can be used whole, crushed, lightly
toasted or dry-fried to release their aroma and
enhance their pungent spiciness, or ground to a fine

Mustard

Hemp

Coriander

Caraway

powder. They are often added ground or whole to curries, chutneys and pickles, especially in Indian cookery. The whole seeds are used for flavouring vinegar for pickled vegetables, and are sometimes added to sausages in some Central European countries.

Ground coriander is an essential component in garam masala as well as the North African fiery red harissa paste. You can also add the crushed seeds to Mexican salsa and guacamole.

It's always best to buy the whole seeds and grind them yourself rather than buy the ready-ground powder, which soon loses its colour and flavour. Better still, grow some coriander (cilantro) plants in your herb bed, patio pots or even a window box and harvest the seeds yourself. Their potency, flavour and aroma will be much more intense than those of bought seeds.

Hemp *Cannabis sativa*

Although the plant from which hemp seeds are gathered is called Cannabis, it is not the same plant as marijuana, which is another member of the same species. With their mild, nutty flavour, the little greenish-white seeds are nutrient-dense and a great source of healthy plant protein. The seeds you buy in the health-food store are actually the soft inner kernels that are removed from the fruits' hard outer casing. The plant is hardy and will grow in a variety of locations, soils and weather conditions.

Hemp plants have been grown for thousands of years in China as a food staple, but throughout the world they were traditionally cultivated for their fibre, used especially in rope-making, rather than as a food source. Nowadays their industrial uses also include plastics, paper production and pet foods. In the United States all varieties of the plant are classed as illegal, even those grown for their seeds or for industrial purposes, so hemp seeds are imported from other countries such as China and Canada.

High in protein and omega fatty acids (they have a perfect balance of omega-3 and -6), and with all 9 essential amino acids, hemp seeds are nutritional powerhouses. As little as two heaped tablespoons contain a staggering 10 grams of protein, making them an important food for vegetarians. They can help to promote a healthy immune system and good bowel function, to prevent constipation and expel toxins from the body, to reduce inflammation and the risk of heart disease, and to lower cholesterol and blood pressure. They also contain several essential minerals, notably iron, zinc, magnesium and phosphorus. Because they are so easily digestible, they are also ideal for people who may be allergic to some other seeds. What they won't do is make you high as, unlike marijuana, they don't contain the psychoactive substance THC (delta-9-tetrahydrocannabinol). Research is being carried out into whether the seeds, due to their high concentrations of healthy fatty acids, may help protect against dementia and degenerative brain diseases and be useful in treating them.

Hemp seeds can be cold-pressed to extract their oil, which can be used in salad dressings and for drizzling over griddled vegetables and pasta. The seeds can be eaten raw, scattered on muesli, yoghurt or salad, or made into hemp seed milk (similar to nut milks) or added to baked savoury dishes, seed cakes and breads.

When buying and eating hemp seeds, check the sell-by dates carefully, as the oil they contain can go rancid quite quickly. Always store them sealed in a cool place.

Mustard *Brassica nigra* (black),

Brassica juncea (brown), *Brassica hirta* (white)
These little round seeds vary in colour from pale yellow (the 'white' seeds) through brown to black. As well as being widely used for the production of mustard and also in pickling, these seeds are a traditional ingredient in many Indian and South Asian curries, chutneys and garnishes, providing heat and a distinctive spicy flavour.

The black seeds are the most pungent and fiery of all, followed by the brown (used in making Dijon mustard), while the white ones (used in American mustard or blended with brown for English mustard) are relatively mild.

To make mustard, the ground seeds are mixed with water or vinegar and can be flavoured with other spices, herbs, honey and seasonings. As well as their uses as a condiment, the seeds can be pressed for their oil, and the green leaves of the plant are edible, too.

Mustard seeds can be traced back almost 5,000 years in Sanskrit and Sumerian texts, and feature in stories about the Buddha as well as the New Testament parable when Jesus compares the Kingdom of Heaven to a mustard seed. The plants were cultivated by the ancient Indus civilization as well as the Greeks and Romans. Most of the mustard seed produced today comes from Nepal and Canada, but it is also grown commercially in India, Europe, the United States and South America.

Mustard seeds are a rich source of nutrients, contributing to a healthy gut and gastrointestinal lining. Their high levels of selenium support the immune system and can improve thyroid function, and, together with magnesium, they have an anti-inflammatory effect, which can be useful to people who suffer from asthma or rheumatoid arthritis. The seeds contain calcium, copper, iron, manganese and zinc as well as being particularly high in B-complex vitamins, especially thiamine, or vitamin B1, which is essential for cellular energy production.

Mustard seeds can be dry-roasted or pan-fried in a little oil until they pop to release their spicy flavour and aroma. They can be added to salad dressings, stirred through steamed or boiled rice, or folded through natural yoghurt with some chilli flakes and curry leaves for a soothing raita to serve with curries. You can add them to fruity raw vegetable slaws and even homemade popcorn.

And don't forget that it's so easy to sprout the seeds (see page 40) by soaking, draining and spreading them between some damp kitchen paper (towel) or cloths. You'll have your own peppery mustard cress for mixing into salads.

Uses & values: seeds within fruits

Alfalfa *Medicago sativa*

The tiny alfalfa seeds are harvested from the fruits of a perennial flowering plant in the Fabaceae legume family. These drought-resistant plants are grown in temperate climates all over the world especially for hay-making, silage and grazing for livestock. In some countries alfalfa is better known as lucerne. The plant looks similar to clover with purple flowers that die off to leave the fruits containing the seeds.

The earliest signs of alfalfa have been found in Persia (now Iran), grown there by the Medes, and from there it spread to ancient Greece and throughout the Roman Empire. The Spanish conquistadors took the seeds across the Atlantic to North and South America to feed their horses, and alfalfa is still grown on the West Coast.

Alfalfa is so rich in nutrients that its Arabic name means 'father of all foods'. Like other seeds, it contains plant protein plus a jackpot of vitamins: A, B, C, D, E and K, and minerals including calcium, magnesium, manganese, copper, phosphorus, zinc and iron. The sprouts are anti-inflammatory, good for cardiovascular health, and contain an enzyme called betaine that plays a role in breaking down proteins and fats in your body. It's beneficial for women, especially during menopause, as it contains plant oestrogens and aids hormonal balance.

The raw, nutty-tasting sprouts taste fabulous in crunchy salads, with hummus, dark-green leafy vegetables such as raw kale and spinach, or with buttery avocado. Use them as an attractive garnish or add them to salad fillings in pitta bread or wraps. They can be stir-fried for a few seconds, but most cooking methods cause them to shrivel and soften unappetizingly, so they're best enjoyed raw.

Cardamom *Elettaria cardamomum, Amomum subulatum*

These delicately flavoured small black seeds are obtained from the light-green pods of the elettaria plant and the brown pods of the amomum species, which are both native to southern Asia, especially India, Pakistan, Bangladesh and Indonesia. The Greek botanist Theophrastus recognized the two plant species and their Indian origins back in the fourth century BC. The name is derived from the Greek word *kardamomon* and the earliest record of this spice appears on ancient Mycenaean tablets.

The seeds contain protein, vitamins A, B-6, B-12, C and D plus an array of minerals including iron, potassium, calcium, copper and magnesium. Cardamom has a warming effect on the body – invigorating and therapeutic. Ayurvedic medical practitioners use the seeds and their oil to calm the mind, relieve tension, and improve memory and concentration. They are anti-spasmodic, anti-inflammatory and good for your gut: settling your stomach, stimulating appetite and helping to create an acidic/alkaline balance in the digestive tract.

They can be used as a natural remedy for many common health complaints. Add them to milky drinks, desserts and rice pudding to act as an expectorant, reducing phlegm and clearing sinuses. Use them as a 'pick-me-up' when you're feeling run down or fatigued, or to help treat urinary tract infections. They can even be chewed after a meal to aid digestion and sweeten the breath.

Cardamom is among the world's most expensive and prized spices. Aromatic and fragrant, the seeds have a highly distinctive taste. Ground into powder, they are often combined with other spices in garam

Vanilla seed

Vanilla pod (bean)

Cumin

Fenugreek

Pomegranate

Nigella

Cardamom

Alfalfa

masala, curry mixes and Thai curry paste. They can also be used whole in lentil dishes and stews or to flavour plain boiled rice and pilaf. They are equally good in sweet dishes and desserts, ranging from traditional Indian sweetmeats, especially kulfi, to Scandinavian sweet breads and even chocolate cake, mousse and ice cream. In India the seeds are used for making tea, while in Israel and some Arab countries they are ground with coffee to make a fragrant hot drink.

Always buy the pods if you can, and avoid any that are discoloured or spotted. To extract the seeds, split open the pods with a small knife, then crush the seeds with a pestle and mortar.

Cumin *Cuminum cyminum*

Ridged, yellowish-brown cumin seeds are encased in the ovoid dried fruits of a slender-stemmed plant in the parsley family. This flowering herb is native to a large swathe of land extending from the eastern Mediterranean through the Middle East to India.

The seed's name is derived from a Greek word, *kyminon*. The earliest mention is in Mycenaean script. From this came the Arabic *kammun* and the Latin *cuminum*. Cumin is grown in countries as diverse as China, Mexico, Chile, Egypt, Morocco, Iran, Uzbekistan and India (the world's biggest producer). It is beloved in Morocco where the seeds are sprinkled on a wide range of foods as a condiment. In India it is often blended with other spices to make curry powder and garam masala.

Cumin seeds add fibre to the diet and encourage a healthy gut and good digestion. They contain phytochemicals – natural plant compounds – carotenes and lutein, which are antioxidant and relieve flatulence. They are a good source of vitamins A, B-complex and C as well as minerals including copper and iron for red blood cells and immune function, zinc for healthy growth and healing wounds, and selenium for protecting cells from damage. The seeds may also have anti-carcinogenic properties; research is ongoing into this possibility.

The warm flavour of cumin with its peppery tones enhances many classic Middle Eastern, Moroccan, Indian and Mexican dishes. You can make the seeds into a soothing tea, sprinkle them on rice, quinoa and grilled (broiled) vegetables, or add them to stews and spicy tagines with chicken or lamb and dried fruits. They are essential in many Indian curries, dhals and masalas. In Mexico, they are often mixed with chilli powder or flakes as a coating for chicken.

The earthy flavour of cumin seeds complements the sweetness of carrots and root vegetables. You can also toast them and add them to a fragrant mustardy vinaigrette for dressing salads. Ground cumin is great in spice mixes, such as za'atar with sumac and sesame seeds.

It is better to buy the seeds than the powder and to grind them yourself. Unlike the powder, the seeds will stay fresh for up to a year.

Fenugreek *Trigonella foenum-graecum*

The fenugreek plant, a leguminous herb, is grown across India and southern Asia, the Middle East, North Africa, France, Spain and Argentina. Similar to clover, it thrives in semi-arid conditions and is used to feed livestock as well as people. Every part of the plant is edible: the leaves are used as a herb or vegetable and the golden amber-coloured seeds as a spice or for sprouts. They are most common in Indian dishes but also widely eaten in Iran, Turkey, Egypt and Ethiopia.

Fenugreek seeds are found inside long yellowish-brown pods and resemble small gritty stones. They are high in protein and a good source of A, B and C vitamins, iron, copper, selenium, zinc, manganese, magnesium and calcium. They can help alleviate digestive problems, relieve constipation, increase the production of breast milk in nursing mothers and contribute to lower blood-sugar levels, which makes them attractive to people with diabetes.

With their pungent, bitter flavour, which is reminiscent of maple syrup, the seeds need to be dry-roasted before being used sparingly. Ground fenugreek is often present in Indian curry powders. Add the seeds to curries, spicy pickles and chutneys, or sprout them and mix into salads with a sweet dressing to counteract their slightly bitter flavour.

Nigella *Nigella sativa*

These little black seeds, which are also known as kalonji, black caraway, black cumin, Roman coriander and black onion seeds, are enclosed in the fruit of the nigella plant, which is native to southern Asia. They have been eaten since ancient times and are used widely throughout India and the Middle East as a flavouring for curries, chicken, lentil and vegetable dishes and even bread.

Nigella seeds have long been prized for their healing properties and are now being hailed as the new wonder seeds. They contain essential omega-3 fats, minerals and dietary fibre and help promote

healthy digestion. Recent research has shown that the seeds are also the repository of a unique plant chemical called thymoquinone, which is anti-inflammatory, anti-parasitic and can help reduce the proliferation of mutant cells in the body. Studies suggest that these seeds can also help reduce blood pressure and type 2 diabetes-associated cholesterol.

The seeds impart a peppery, onion-like flavour, which is pungent and slightly bitter, and they are best dry-fried before they're used. Crushing them releases their mild peppery aroma. If you want to grind them yourself, use a spice mill or coffee mill – it's hard work with a pestle and mortar. You can add them to dhal, vegetables, chutneys, pickles and naan bread. In North Africa, bakers add them to a variety of white breads. Sprinkle them over steamed rice, scrambled eggs, roasted carrots and parsnips, and raw tomatoes, or stir them into a salad dressing.

Pomegranate *Punica granatum*

For many years we have enjoyed pomegranates as a rather unusual fruit, but it's only recently that we have started to recognize their myriad health and nutritional benefits. The hundreds of edible seeds, or arils, are immediately visible when you cut open the ripe fruits, which grow on small trees and shrubs around the Mediterranean, Asia, the Indian subcontinent and tropical Africa.

With its origins in ancient Persia, the pomegranate's name is derived from the Latin for a seeded apple. The seeds can be eaten raw, juiced or made into a syrup or pomegranate molasses. They are a good source of dietary fibre and help digestion and a healthy bowel. In addition to minerals, B-complex vitamins and vitamins C and K, the seeds contain compounds that could help reduce heart disease, improve circulation and help protect cells from some cancers. Eating them regularly can also boost your immune system.

Pomegranates are a staple of Middle Eastern food, especially traditional Persian dishes such as fesenjan (stewed chicken and walnuts in pomegranate juice) and saffron pilaf with pomegranate seeds. They are also used extensively in North African desserts, where they are often teamed with rose water.

To extract the seeds: cut a pomegranate in half horizontally and hold each half, cut-side down, over a large bowl. Hit the skin hard with a rolling pin to release the seeds into the bowl. Add them to tagines and stews – they go well with pork, duck and chicken – or mix them with salty feta or creamy mozzarella, sliced oranges and pistachios or pine nuts as an appetizer. Sprinkle them over salads, cooked grains or thick vegetable soups, stir into a fresh tomato salsa with coriander (cilantro) and chilli, or simply scatter some over a bowl of thick Greek yoghurt with a drizzle of honey, some toasted nuts and a pinch of ground cinnamon. Delicious!

Vanilla *Vanilla planifolia*

Vanilla is one of the world's most popular flavourings and aromas and is added to everything from ice cream and cakes to perfume and shower gel. The tiny seeds are like black specks and are enclosed in the long, slender pods (beans) of the tropical climbing vanilla orchid, which has been cultivated in Mexico since pre-Columbian times. Beloved of the Aztecs, it was introduced to Europe by the Spanish in the sixteenth century. Vanilla is expensive partly because the plants have to be pollinated by hand, and growing it is labour intensive.

Vanilla contains small amounts of vitamin B and traces of iron, zinc, calcium, magnesium, potassium and manganese. Because it is eaten in such small quantities, the nutritional and health benefits are probably minimal.

The whole dried vanilla pods (beans) can be used to flavour milk and other liquids by heating them together. Or they can be tucked into a jar of sugar to add their distinctive aroma and flavour – it will take about three weeks to permeate it.

To extract the seeds, slit a pod (bean) open from top to bottom and scrape them out with the point of a sharp knife. Use them in smoothies, cakes, muffins and baking, pancakes, ice cream, custards, sauces and creamy desserts – they will fleck them attractively. Vanilla is often added to savoury dishes, too, and it goes surprisingly well with chicken, duck and seafood. Some people even add a few seeds to chilli con carne.

Uses & values: flower heads & kernels

Fennel *Foeniculum vulgare*

The dried green or light-brown grooved seeds of the perennial fennel herb (a member of the Umbelliferae family) have a distinctive aniseed flavour and sweet aroma. The plant is a native of the Mediterranean region and flourishes in dry soils in coastal areas. Its seeds and feathery leaves were well known to the ancient Greeks who used them for medicinal and culinary purposes. Fennel is now grown all over the world, especially in India and the Middle East, where it is a widely used spice.

The seeds are a good source of dietary fibre, and help promote a healthy digestive system. In some countries, such as India, they are often chewed as a natural digestive and breath freshener after meals, and in traditional medicine they are used as a remedy for indigestion and flatulence. The oil extracted from the seeds is used in gripe water to relieve colic in babies. Fennel seeds contain vitamins A, B-complex, C and E as well as some important minerals, notably iron, manganese, copper, calcium, magnesium and zinc.

Used whole or ground in cooking, the seeds are one of the ingredients in the traditional Chinese five-spice powder mix. In Italy, they are mixed with aromatic herbs and ground spices into pork sausage meat or spicy pork meatballs served in a tomato sauce. The whole or ground seeds are used widely in Indian cookery, too, especially in curry powder mixes, potato and vegetable curries, pickles, chutneys, condiments and as a flavouring for naan bread. The seeds can also be used to flavour bread and pizza dough, pastry (pie crust), cakes, muffins, cookies and biscotti. You can even add them to ice cream and nutty pralines. They taste great in salad dressings, especially drizzled over raw sliced fennel bulb or combined with fresh orange. And they can scent a simple pork or lamb joint roasted in the oven with potatoes, fresh herbs, olive oil and lemon.

Fennel seeds are the principal ingredients in many fragrant tisanes as well as the Indian masala tea, and are especially good in winter when they may be helpful in relieving coughs and congested sinuses. Drinking a cup of soothing fennel tea can also aid digestion and reduce bloating and flatulence.

Fennel seeds stay fresh for longer than most other seeds and will keep for up to two years if stored in an airtight container in a cool, dark place.

Poppy *Papaver somniferum*

These tiny black or slate-blue seeds, which are less than a millimetre long, are harvested from the dried seed pods of opium poppies. They are safe to eat and have a very low opiate content with no narcotic effects. They are beloved of classic Eastern and Central European cooking where they are added whole or as a paste to seed cakes, pies, bread and cheesecake. The seeds can be pressed for their oil, or ground to an oily paste.

Poppies have been cultivated since ancient times for their seeds, which were thought to have supernatural powers and used as natural remedies. The Minoans and the Egyptians employed them as a sedative and to combat insomnia.

Although they are usually eaten in very small quantities, poppy seeds pack quite a nutritional punch and are vitamin and mineral rich, especially in B-complex vitamins, manganese, copper, iron and calcium. They contain fatty oleic acid, which helps to

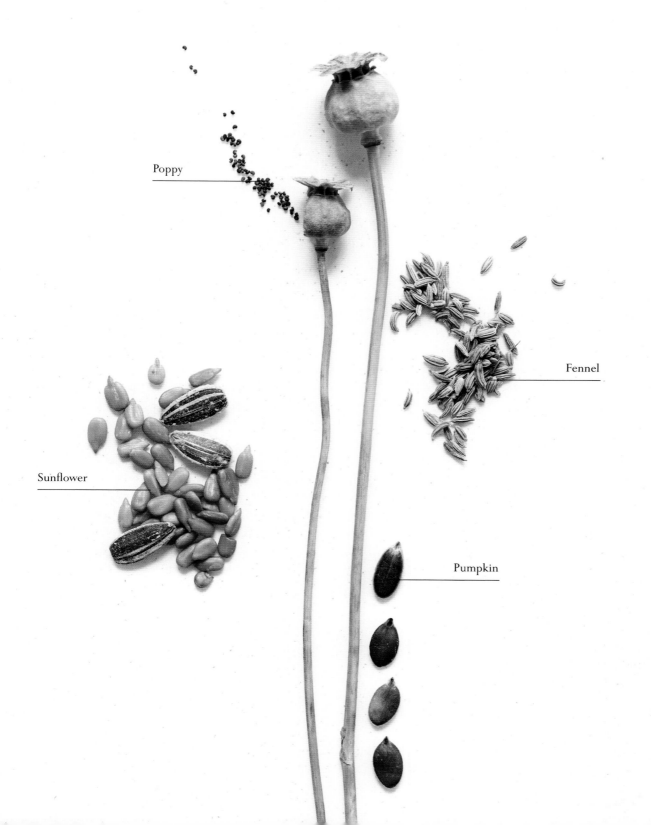

Poppy

Fennel

Sunflower

Pumpkin

increase 'good' cholesterol (HDL) and lower 'bad' cholesterol (LDL) levels in the body.

Poppy seeds are traditionally used for sprinkling over crackers, bagels, hamburger buns and white bread, or mixing into muffin and cake batters. They can also be added to pastry (pie-crust) dough and cheesecake crumb bases. Mix them into poached or stewed fruit for strudels and pies. In India, they are sometimes used in sweets or as a garnish for desserts, or they are dry-fried with spices and coconut and added to kormas or mixed into cooked rice, potato and vegetable dishes. You can stir them into salad dressings or sprinkle them over roast chicken, griddled prawns (shrimp) and roasted vegetables to add a slightly gritty texture and earthy flavour. Like other seeds, they can be roasted on a baking (cookie) sheet in the oven or quickly dry-fried in a shallow frying pan (skillet) to intensify their slightly nutty taste and aroma.

Poppy seeds can turn rancid relatively quickly so always check the sell-by date on packets before you buy, and store them carefully. They should stay fresh for up to six months.

Pumpkin *Cucurbita pepo*

Often known by their Spanish name 'pepitas', especially in Mexico and the United States, pumpkin seeds are oval, flat and dark-green. Pumpkins are native to the Americas and have been grown there as domestic crops for thousands of years. In the United States, piles of freshly harvested pumpkins are stacked for sale along country roads in the autumn (fall) in readiness for Halloween and Thanksgiving, when spiced pumpkin pie is the traditional dessert. Each ripe pumpkin contains hundreds of seeds enclosed in pale yellowish husks, which you can scoop out of the centre and dry. They have a high fat content and their intensely nutty-flavoured oil can be extracted by pressing the hulled roasted seeds. It is used in Eastern Europe for dressing salads and for drizzling over cooked vegetables and pumpkin soup.

Pumpkin seeds are nutrient dense and a good source of protein and dietary fibre. They contain vitamins B, C, E and K plus an array of minerals – calcium, iron, copper, manganese, magnesium, phosphorus, potassium and especially zinc, which plays an important role in breaking down carbohydrates in the body, cell growth and a healthy immune system.

The seeds have a sweet nutty taste and crunchy texture. They are often roasted (sometimes with spices or salt added) and served as snacks and street food, particularly in Mexico, the United States and Greece. Add them to pasta bakes, stir-fries and salads, or sprinkle them over cereal, fruit or yoghurt for a healthy breakfast. Mix them into homemade muesli, granola and breakfast bars, bread or cookie dough, flapjacks, sweet and savoury muffins and pancake batters. Grind and add them to citrusy salad dressings or even veggie-burgers. The whole seeds, raw or roasted, also make a colourful garnish for thick puréed vegetable soups. Add them to homemade trail mixes with dried fruit, toasted nuts and banana chips.

The Aztecs ground their pumpkin seeds with fresh chillies and other spices to create savoury sauces. You can make a fiery version of pesto in the same way to serve with fish, chicken, pasta and grilled (broiled) vegetables. Blitz some roasted seeds in a food processor or blender with garlic, fresh coriander (cilantro), spring onions (scallions), tomatoes, lime juice, olive oil and grated Parmesan cheese. Or just grind the seeds and add them to a spicy tomato salsa to serve with Mexican dishes such as fajitas, nachos, wraps and tacos.

Roasting or dry-frying the seeds will bring out their natural flavour and aroma. For spicy seeds, try adding a little chilli powder, paprika or cumin to them before roasting; or drizzle with honey for a sweet flavour. Alternatively, you can toast them and serve them warm as a snack with drinks, sprinkled with some soy sauce.

Pumpkin seeds can be sprouted, and impart a wonderful taste and texture to dark-green leafy salads made with spinach and shredded kale.

Sunflower *Helianthus annuus*

Sunflower seeds are the edible kernels in the black or grey-and-white striped husks that form in the sunflower head as it starts to dry out after flowering. Sunflowers are grown commercially mostly for their oil, which is extracted by pressing the seeds. They originated in Central America (Peru and Mexico) and have been cultivated for over 2,000 years by Native Americans. The seeds were brought to Europe by the Spanish and now these beautiful plants are grown all over the world.

Nutritionally, the seeds are a rich source of protein and dietary fibre. They are quite high in energy, as their fat content (polyunsaturated) is over 50 per cent. They also contain vitamins E and B-complex and are a rich source of folic acid, which is important for women during pregnancy. The seeds are also a good source of several minerals including iron, zinc, selenium, calcium, potassium, magnesium and manganese, which play a role in producing hormones, red blood cells, strong bones and healthy muscles.

The nutty-tasting seeds, salted and roasted in their shells, are sometimes sold as snacks. Or you can dry-fry them or toast them with ground spices to enhance their aroma. Use the shelled ones in dukka and other crunchy sprinkles for salads, cereal and yoghurt, or bake with them – they add flavour and texture to seedy bread, cakes, cookies, power bars, pancakes and cheesecake bases. Add them to muesli and granola or even to a crumble topping for baked fruit.

Uses & values: pseudocereals

Buckwheat *Fagopyrum esculentum*

This plant's name is misleading as it is not a member of the wheat family nor a grass or cereal, but actually a member of the rhubarb family. However, it is grown commercially as a grain and can be ground into a dark-coloured flour or made into noodles. Each triangular greenish-brown seed or 'groat' is enclosed within a dark outer hull.

Buckwheat originated in southeast Asia about 8,000 years ago. Cultivation spread from China and Tibet to central Asia and the Balkans. It is popular in Russia where it has been consumed as a staple for hundreds of years and forms the basis of many national dishes, notably *kasha*.

One of the reasons for the recent surge in buckwheat's popularity in Western countries – where it was not eaten traditionally – is that it is gluten-free, making it a healthy alternative to wheat for people with gluten intolerance and coeliac disease. It is a good source of protein and dietary fibre as well as vitamins B and C, and has a high mineral content, including magnesium, manganese, phosphorus, zinc, iron and potassium. Buckwheat is rich in flavonoids, which enable vitamin C to help protect against infections and disease. Ongoing research is studying whether it can be used as a tool to manage diabetes by lowering blood glucose levels.

Although buckwheat is filling, it is very low in fat (only 3.5 per cent) and reduces food cravings, which makes it a good choice for people on weight-reduction and -maintenance regimes. It also contains rutin, a nutrient that helps strengthen the walls of the micro-capillaries, thereby improving circulation and helping to protect against cardio-vascular and brain diseases.

Unroasted buckwheat has a more subtle flavour than the roasted variety which tends to be more nutty and smoky tasting. Buckwheat is versatile and can be made into a delicious 'porridge', flavoured with ground cinnamon and served with fresh fruit, honey and yoghurt, or added to soups, stews and casseroles. Because of its earthy flavour, mushrooms, root vegetables and cabbage all go well with buckwheat. A popular way of eating the roasted variety is to make a pilaf with it, which can be eaten hot as a side dish or cooled and mixed with vegetables, nuts, herbs and vinaigrette for a healthy salad. Or try stir-frying the cooked groats with ginger, shredded vegetables, chilli and sesame seeds and oil. The raw groats can be sprouted and added to salads.

The flour may be light- or dark-coloured and is used in baking cakes, muffins, bread, crackers, pancakes, blinis and galettes as well as for making noodles. In India, pakoras are often made with buckwheat flour and it is used for coating vegetables before frying them. In some parts of Italy the flour substitutes for potato or semolina in gnocchi. Buckwheat can be eaten Japanese-style with soba noodles, served cold with a dipping sauce, added to soup, or tossed warm in a salad with a spicy Thai or sesame dressing.

Chia *Salvia hispanica*

These tiny oval mottled seeds, which may be black or white, come from a herb in the mint family. What makes them special is their hydrophilicity – their ability to absorb water: they swell up to 15 times their original size when soaked, acquiring an unusual gel-like consistency. The distinctive round gelatinous

Red quinoa   White quinoa   Black sesame   White sesame

Buckwheat   Linseed   Chia

globules resemble tapioca. They have a rather bland but slightly nutty flavour, and can be pressed to extract their oil.

Chia is native to Mexico where it has been cultivated for thousands of years as a staple food crop and was regarded as sacred by the Aztecs, who are known to have used it in medicines and religious ceremonies. It is now grown throughout South America and Australia.

The seeds are regarded as a superfood since they can help lower cholesterol and reduce the risk of heart disease. They are rich in vitamin B-complex, especially niacin and thiamine, which release energy from carbohydrates and help maintain cellular and organ function. They also contain vitamins A, C and E plus minerals, including manganese, magnesium, calcium, iron and zinc. They are a good source of

plant protein, having all the essential amino acids, and dietary fibre, and contain omega-3 fatty acids.

The raw seeds can be sprinkled on cereals, yoghurt and salads or added to bread, cakes, energy bars, granola, oatmeal and dips. Use them whole or ground in smoothies and juices, or make them into a delicious gelatinous porridge.

Linseed *Linum usitatissimum*

Linseed is flaxseed: different names for the same seed, which is derived from the flax plant. Flax is better known for producing textiles (linen) and linseed oil, which is used for finishing and treating wood as well as a nutritional supplement. Flax has been grown for thousands of years in the Middle East and Egypt where linen was used by the Romans for sailmaking.

The reddish-brown or golden yellow seeds are a good source of protein, omega-3 fatty acids, vitamins B and C, and minerals, especially magnesium, phosphorus, zinc, iron and calcium. Due to their high fibre content, they have long been recognized as a natural remedy for relieving constipation. The seeds can be pressed to extract a rich, buttery-tasting oil that can be used as a laxative. Ground or roasted linseed can be soaked in water to release a gum (similar to xanthan gum), which can be used in gluten-free baking.

You can add the mild, nutty-flavoured seeds to bread, cakes, muffins, pancakes, waffles, power bars, crackers, muesli and porridge. They are best freshly ground rather than left whole as this makes them easier to digest – use a small spice or coffee mill. Alternatively, you can soak linseed in water overnight and add the swollen seeds to breakfast fruit juices or smoothies. In India, the seeds are sometimes added to curries, chutneys and raita or ground and mixed with chapati flour to make roti.

The oil can be whisked with other ingredients in salad dressings, stirred into cooked rice or drizzled over griddled and roasted vegetables. It should not be used for cooking as it can be rendered unstable and burn at relatively low temperatures.

Quinoa *Chenopodium quinoa*
Pronounced 'keen-wah', this pseudocereal originated in the Andes in South America where it was grown by the Incas for food. It's not a true grass or cereal and it is cultivated primarily for its seeds, which are housed within the dried seed heads on the stalks. It thrives in a cool climate at high altitude and can withstand low temperatures. Once a staple food in Peru, Ecuador, Bolivia, Colombia and Chile, it is now eaten all over the world and grown in North America and Europe, too.

The seeds are cooked and eaten whole or can be ground into flour for gluten-free baking and pasta-making. Most of the quinoa we buy is white. Black and red varieties are available, too, but they have a slightly more crunchy texture and take a little longer to cook.

Quinoa is a good source of protein and contains all the essential amino acids. It is gluten free and easy to digest, very low in fat and contains vitamins A, B, C and E as well as potassium, phosphorus, manganese, iron, zinc, calcium and magnesium.

Cooked quinoa has a slightly bitter, nutty flavour, a fluffy texture with a little crunch and translucent appearance, and it bulks up to four times its original volume. It is prepared in a similar way to rice and should be rinsed thoroughly before being cooked. Bring to the boil, then simmer for about 20 minutes. It's ready to eat when the seed separates from the germ and appears to sprout a 'tail', and is still slightly firm to the bite (al dente). Cover the pan and stand for 8–10 minutes before stirring and serving.

It can be mixed with vegetables, herbs, spices, nuts and fruit, such as pomegranate seeds, and dressed to make a filling salad or used in a stuffing for vegetables, meat and poultry. You can add it to veggie-burger mixes, serve it with stews or roast chicken, grilled (broiled) fish and prawns (shrimp), or make it into a Middle Eastern pilaf, tabbouleh or Indian-style pilau. It tastes delicious just served hot and dressed simply with some olive oil and lemon or lime juice with a grinding of black pepper and sea salt. Stir in a few chopped herbs for extra flavour.

Try simmering quinoa in coconut milk for an unusual alternative to breakfast cereal, or add it to oatmeal and serve with cinnamon and fruit. You can even bake bread and cookies with it, or sprout it (*see page 40*) and mix the sprouts into salads.

Sesame *Sesamum indicum*

The sesame plant, which originated in India, will tolerate drought conditions and intense heat, and has been grown in tropical regions for thousands of years for its edible seeds and the oil they yield. The small seeds, which are usually white or black, grow in fruit capsules called pods. Most of the world's sesame crop today is grown in India, China and Nigeria.

Sesame seeds are high in healthy mono-unsaturated fat (50 per cent), which helps to lower blood cholesterol. They are good sources of protein and dietary fibre, vitamins A, B-complex, C and E as well as copper, manganese, magnesium, iron, zinc and calcium. They are particularly rich in selenium, an important mineral that helps support the immune system, sex glands and optimal functioning of the thyroid gland, which regulates metabolism, and heat and weight levels in the body. Many health claims are made for these remarkable little seeds, and they are used to help treat and relieve a range of conditions from diabetes and high blood pressure to gingivitis.

The distinctive rich, nutty flavour of sesame is prized throughout a wide range of cuisines from India, South Asia, Japan, China, Vietnam, the Levant and Eastern Mediterranean to the Caribbean, Mexico and the United States. The seeds are versatile and can be used in sprinkles, toppings, garnishes and decorations for bread, burger buns, cakes, crackers, sushi and salads. They can be used to coat chicken, salmon and tuna before baking (try mixing them with soy sauce, garlic, honey and sesame oil), added with miso to soba noodle dishes, or stirred into cooked rice with chilli and spices, or added to stir-fries. They are used to flavour Indian spicy vegetable dishes, condiments, chutneys, pickles and sweetmeats. In Greece and the Caribbean, they are made into brittle sweet bars and added to desserts, while in Mexico they give a nutty taste to savoury moles and flatbreads. Throughout the Middle East, North Africa, Central and Eastern Europe they are mixed with honey or sugar to make halva, a dense sweet tablet that is served in thin slices.

Probably the best-known food made from toasted ground sesame seeds is tahini. This thick paste, which is a staple of Levantine and eastern Mediterranean cooking, is used for flavouring hummus and grilled (broiled) aubergine (eggplant) dishes as well as a base for sauces, dressings and dips. You can buy it in jars in most supermarkets and delis or make it yourself by blitzing toasted sesame seeds and oil in a food processor to a smooth, thick pouring consistency. It will keep in a sealed jar in the refrigerator for several months.

Sesame oil is used in many Chinese, Japanese, Korean, Vietnamese and Indian dishes. Fragrant and aromatic, it is usually sprinkled over food just before serving or used in dressings for cooked vegetables and salads but you can cook with it, too. You can also buy toasted sesame oil, which is darker and more intensely flavoured. It has a longer shelf life than the regular sesame oil.

In Ayurvedic medicine, sesame oil is used for massage, especially for babies and infants.

Uses & values: at a glance

This chart of seeds and their properties sets out the particular benefits that each seed type offers, so it will help you identify which of them could be especially useful to you in addressing any specific susceptibilities, as well as supporting your general health and well-being.

At a glance: fruits

SEED	DESCRIPTION	CULINARY USES	NUTRIENTS	BENEFITS
CARAWAY	Dark-brown seeds found in umbels (umbrella-like fruits emanating from a central stem) in the creamy white flowers of the biennial plant.	Roasted or toasted lightly to release their aroma, they are most frequently used in flatbreads, cakes, cheeses and some meat dishes for their spicy aromas.	Antioxidant vitamins A, C, E, zinc and manganese, and nutrients lutein, carotene and zeoxanthin; as well as calcium, magnesium, potassium and the B vitamins, plus various essential oils.	Anti-spasmodic, used to help relieve flatulence and indigestion, infantile colic, and can help protect the colon from potential cancers.
CORIANDER	The mature plant bears small light-pink flowers that turn into oval fruits. When dried in the sun for a few days, these become the seeds.	Crushed and lightly roasted or toasted, they are used in curries and other Asian-style dishes, and to flavour meats and fish for BBQ, salads, dressings, sauces and marinades. Also used in grain-based dishes (barley, wild and black rices).	Iron, copper, calcium, magnesium, manganese, zinc, oleic and palmitic essential fats, as well as omega-6. High in vitamin C and vitamin K.	Bone and ligament health, powerful antioxidants helping to lower LDL cholesterol (low-density lipo-protein). Fibre helps to keep colon clean. Zinc for sperm health. Essential fats for skin.
HEMP	The small, greenish-white seed is the fruit of the male plant, found in spiky clusters at the centre of small green flowers.	Used for its oil in dressings and marinades, also as sprouted seeds for salads, and sprinkles for soups. Now also used in grain-based dishes such as barley, wild and black rices.	All 20 known amino acids, which help break down elements of protein. Seeds contain cannabinoids (or CBD), the nutrient that's also contained in cannabis; B vitamins, niacin, thiamine and riboflavin. Essential fatty acids, omega-3 and -6.	Can help blood sugar control, reducing inflammation, lowering blood pressure, hormone-regulating, high protein assimilation for growth, healing and repair. Potent anti-inflammatory, anti-convulsive and pain-relieving effects; can help with the production of cell energy.
MUSTARD	Found in the fruit pods that develop on the flowers of the mustard greens as they ripen. They may be 'white' (pale yellow), brown or black, and have differing levels of spice according to colour.	Roasted, or dry-toasted and ground finely to a powder, added to other spices to create sprinkles and flavourings for meat, fish, some grain dishes and vegetables. Powder may also be added to dressings and marinades for poultry, meat and fish.	Especially rich in selenium, a mineral known for its immune-supporting properties; magnesium, manganese, phosphorus, copper, vitamin B1 thiamine and fibre.	Boosts immunity, helps balance hormones, relieves symptoms of menopause, improves sleep, anti-asthmatic and helps relieve inflammation relating to rheumatoid arthritis.

At a glance: seeds within fruits

SEED	DESCRIPTION	CULINARY USES	NUTRIENTS	BENEFITS
ALFALFA	The smallest of all the seeds in this group, they are found in the perennial crop of a purple-flowering plant that comes from the pea family.	Mainly sprouted for use in salads, to adorn soups and dress fish and meat dishes.	All the antioxidants that other larger seeds contain, and in particular the full range of B vitamins that are essential for energy production, as well as abundant minerals, calcium, magnesium, manganese, zinc and copper. These are found most abundantly when the seeds are sprouted (see pages 40–41).	Energy, healing and repair; regeneration of all vital organs.
CARDAMOM	The tiny seeds are arranged in vertical rows (sometimes known as arils) found in the cardamom fruit.	The fruit and its seeds are often eaten whole in India, but in Western cooking added to dishes for their pungent flavour, and then removed once cooked. Used in warm milk and milk puddings, rice dishes both sweet and savoury.	Calcium, magnesium, potassium, antioxidants, vitamins B and C.	Immune-supportive, they reduce phlegm in the bronchial tract (nose, throat, chest), helping to clear chest infections, and calm digestion. Anti-inflammatory.
CUMIN	Grey-yellow oblong-shaped seeds, they come from the dried fruit pod of the cumin plant, which is part of the parsley family. Often confused with fennel seeds, cumin seeds are far more spicy.	As seeds or ground into fine powder, cumin is used in many Indian and Persian dishes, both vegetarian and animal-based, as well as rice, beverages and sweet condiments.	Packed with antioxidants, vitamins A, C and E, all of which work together; zinc and selenium, as well as potassium, calcium, magnesium and manganese.	Bone health, eye health, cardiovascular-supporting, lowering blood pressure, aiding digestion, reducing flatulence, anti-microbial, anti-fungal.
FENUGREEK	Ochre-coloured, tiny di-cotyledons (two-sided, as in a broad bean), the seeds are found in the dried fruit of the fenugreek herb.	Used as spice in vegetables, salads, grain dishes, marinades, poultry and fish dishes.	Fibre, copper, iron, selenium and zinc, vitamins A and C, B-complex, and folate.	Helps balance blood-sugar level by supporting the production of insulin; supports digestion, and heart/cardiovascular health.

SEED	DESCRIPTION	CULINARY USES	NUTRIENTS	BENEFITS
NIGELLA	Small angular black seeds found in the annual pale-blue or white flower of the plant as the dried fruit capsule releases the seeds.	Used with fruits, vegetables, salads, poultry and curries.	The seed oils contain a type of essential fat known as conjugated linoleic acid (CLA), which can be helpful for weight loss, and helps neutralize potentially damaging saturated fats.	Weight management/loss, heart and brain health, cellular energy production, hormone balance.
POMEGRANATE	Pink, juicy seeds found within the fruits of the same name, protected by pithy white flesh.	Adds sweet, juicy flavour and crunchy texture to breakfast bowls and pancakes, juices, smoothies and salads, and decoration for many main dishes.	Protein, fibre, essential fats, beta-carotene, flavanols and polyphenols, vitamin C and punicalagins (all of which are potent antioxidants, essential for mopping up debris in the body caused by natural metabolic functions), vitamin K for blood clotting.	Weight loss, anti-inflammatory, potent antioxidant for the immune system, can help provide protection against Alzheimer's and other brain-related diseases, as well as prostate and breast cancers. Can help lower blood pressure, balance good:bad HDL:LDL cholesterol ratios. Anti-bacterial and anti-fungal.
VANILLA	Black seeds found in a pod (bean); the fruit of the only known fruit-bearing orchid.	Can be infused in milks, creams, yoghurts and ice creams, as well as oils and baked dishes.	Calcium, magnesium, potassium and manganese.	Bone and ligament health, hair and nails.

At a glance: flower heads & kernels

SEED	DESCRIPTION	CULINARY USES	NUTRIENTS	BENEFITS
FENNEL	Harvested from the herbaceous fennel plant when their seed heads turn light brown. The seeds are oblong, 3–4mm long, light-brown in colour with fine vertical stripes over their surface.	To enhance their fragrance and flavour, fennel seeds are generally ground just before use, or whole seeds gently toasted. Can be used as a savoury spice, as a condiment or flavouring base. Used widely in fish and vegetable dishes, and in cheese spreads, also to flavour breads and cakes.	Rich source of dietary fibre and abundant antioxidants. Minerals include: copper, iron, calcium, potassium, manganese, selenium, zinc and magnesium. Vitamins A, C and E along with B vitamins 1, 2, 3 and 6.	A remedy for flatulence and indigestion in traditional medicines. Is thought to help increase breast milk production in nursing mothers. Powerful antioxidant, with anti-inflammatory and digestive properties. Helps lower LDL cholesterol levels.
POPPY	Blue-black in colour, and originating from the pods of the brightly coloured flower.	Can enhance salads, baked dishes, dressings and dips. Often used in Persian/Middle Eastern cooking.	Rich in antioxidants, oleic and essential fatty acids, fibre, iron, copper, calcium, manganese, B vitamins.	Lowers LDL (low-density lipo-protein, which is considered damaging) cholesterol. Skin-enhancing, can help ease constipation.
PUMPKIN	Flat, dark-green seeds found inside the gourd (fruit) of the same name. Some are encased in a yellow-white husk/kernel.	Toasted pumpkin seeds can be used to garnish porridge, yoghurt, soups, stir-fries and salads. They can also be used in energy bars and granola. Ground pumpkin seeds make a great coating for meats and poultry.	Manganese, phosphorus, copper, iron, magnesium, zinc, vitamin K and B-complex. High in protein.	Antioxidant support, anti-microbial and supports gut health, prostate health, kidney function and the regulation of insulin production.
SUNFLOWER	Found in the bright yellow, seed-studded centre of the sunflower itself. They are grey-green in colour and turn black when exposed to intense sunlight.	Can be sprouted to add protein and enzymes to salads, soups and juices/smoothies, or roasted/toasted for an increased nutty flavour to add to granola, breakfast cereals, or vegan bites and bars; or blended into dips and spreads.	One of the highest vegetarian sources of protein, fibre and polyunsaturated fats, making the oil second in popularity only to olive oil. Thiamine (B1), niacin (B3), pyridoxine (B6), folate, iron, zinc, phosphorus, copper, potassium, selenium, vitamin E, magnesium and manganese.	Helps to release energy from food by contributing to metabolism function. Anti-inflammatory and beneficial to cardiovascular system, by helping to lower damaging LDL cholesterol. Calms nerves, supports liver detoxification.

At a glance: pseudocereals

SEED	DESCRIPTION	CULINARY USES	NUTRIENTS	BENEFITS
BUCKWHEAT	From the rhubarb family, with a beechnut-like shape and wheat-like characteristics (but without the allergens). The seed has a unique triangular shape and is found at the top of the stem, similar to cereals.	Often served as an alternative to rice or porridge, and as a gluten-free alternative to flour in recipes such as pancakes, muffins and breads.	Manganese, copper, magnesium, phosphorus, B-complex vitamins, soluble and insoluble fibre.	Cardiovascular, linked to lowering cholesterol and high blood pressure. Fibre helps lower risk of diabetes and contributes to blood sugar control. May help prevent gallstones.
CHIA	The seed head grows with the appearance of wheat or barley at the top of the chia stalk, hence the term 'pseudocereal'.	An alternative to oat-based porridge, to wheat, rice or barley in savoury or sweet dishes, as a high-protein ingredient in vegan smoothies and other healthy drinks. Suitable for high-protein diets.	One of the highest vegetable sources of protein, fibre, omega-3, -6, -9, calcium, magnesium, iron, zinc and folic acid.	Digestion, bone health, cognitive function and brain health, energy and vitality.
LINSEED	Linseed comes from the flax plant. In raw form, linseeds range from yellow to reddish-brown in colour. Avoid raw linseeds that are white, green or black in colour as these have been harvested before or after their ideal maturity.	Stir into warm cereals or blend into smoothies. Ground linseed can also be used in pancakes or waffles where it can be substituted for a quarter of the flour. Can be added to salad dressings for a slight nutty flavour.	One of the highest beneficial omega-3:6 essential fatty acid ratios of all seeds. Also contain copper, manganese, magnesium, phosphorus, selenium, B-complex vitamins and fibre.	Antioxidant protection, cardiovascular and anti-inflammatory benefits, supports digestive health; eases PMS and post-menopausal symptoms, and helps to balance hormonal health generally.
QUINOA	From the same family as spinach, Swiss chard and beetroot (beets). The whole plant can be eaten. Seeds can be white, red or black, and may have a translucent appearance when cooked.	Excellent in a gluten-free diet. Can be used in baked goods and as a pasta substitute, chilled in salads, served as a breakfast porridge alternative, added to soups and stews, and is great in tabbouleh.	Manganese, copper, phosphorus, magnesium, zinc, a rich source of folate and fibre. High in protein.	Anti-inflammatory, antioxidant and energy producing; low allergen risk.
SESAME	A flowering plant cultivated for its tiny, flat, oval seeds with a nutty taste and delicate crunch. May be found in a variety of colours including white, yellow, black and red.	Add to bread, muffin or biscuit mixes. Add to steamed broccoli or other green vegetables. Essential for making tahini (see page 51), salad dressings and many Asian-inspired dishes.	Copper, manganese, calcium, magnesium, phosphorus, iron, zinc, molybdenum, selenium, B-complex vitamins and fibre.	Supports bone, vascular and respiratory health and lowers LDL cholesterol. Can help prevent osteoporosis, and reduce migraine and PMS symptoms.

Preparing your seeds

Sowing & growing

You don't have to have elaborate equipment or acres of space to grow your own seeds. A few pots on the kitchen windowsill – and a little bit of patience – are all you need to get started.

The first step is to allocate a space in your home, or outside on a balcony (preferably away from any environmental pollution such as exhaust fumes), in a conservatory or cold-frame, or in a greenhouse if you have one.

Seeds need to be nurtured daily until they are sturdy enough to withstand the elements. Excessive cold, rain and wind can all damage tender plants in the early stages of growth, so make sure you choose a sheltered place with a relatively constant temperature for this initial phase.

The right container

Terracotta pots are ideal for cultivating plants because they absorb and hold moisture, which helps prevent the soil from drying out completely between watering sessions. However you can use any vessel for your seeds provided there are drainage holes in the base to allow excess water to escape. Waterlogged roots will damage or kill your plant just as surely as dried-out compost will.

Garden centres and nurseries can provide seed trays made of compostable material that will allow you to move your tender seedlings undisturbed into larger containers, so protecting their roots. This is especially important for the more delicate seeds such as alfalfa, poppy and sesame. Alternatively, sow seed directly into the pots from which you plan to harvest your crop.

Coriander and fennel seed, for example, tend to grow very quickly, and will flower rapidly if their leaves are not regularly harvested. If they are planted in their own individual pots from the start they can mature without taking over the whole herb garden or kitchen.

I usually sow straight into the containers I will harvest from, but have also sown many new types of seeds in empty egg-boxes, since they provide convenient individual zones as well as the larger flat section of the lid. This works well for the first few weeks, until the seeds have grown their first shoot, at which point they can be moved into the larger containers outside if the weather is mild enough. Pots and containers can be moved around to shield the growing plants from too much sun, rain or wind, and eventually to somewhere convenient when they are mature and ready for cutting/harvesting.

Don't forget the labels

Too many times I have planted seeds and waited patiently for the first sprouts to appear – only to realize I don't know what kind of plant is emerging. It's so tempting to think you will remember which seedling is which, but my advice is not to chance it: label each different type from the start.

There are dozens of kinds of labels available from garden centres and hardware stores, or you can make your own using a permanent marker or non-toxic paint and lolly (popsicle) sticks, clothes pegs (clothes pins), slivers of timber, pebbles, china fragments or even upturned terracotta pots.

Positioning

If you are growing seeds indoors, put them where they are exposed to daylight, and keep them separate from detergents and other household sprays. Make sure there is plenty of fresh air moving through the area where your seeds are growing – as there would be in an outdoor environment – but don't leave them in a draught, as this will stunt their growth.

Growing organically

We encourage you to grow your seeds in the most natural way, so be sure to use organic compost and to avoid synthetic or chemically-enhanced feeds or sprays. Any foodstuffs, including seeds, benefit from being grown in organic compost, not only because of its carefully balanced nutritional content but also because it is free of pesticides, herbicides, added hormones or potentially harmful chemicals. It's as much about what is left out as what is put in. Remember that your seeds are the very start of life, and whatever medium you grow them in will become part of them.

There are increasing numbers of seed companies that pride themselves in supplying original, non-genetically-modified seeds that will grow well given the water, sunlight and seasonal variations they have evolved to flourish in. It may be that because your seeds are not artificially enhanced, some may succumb to adverse weather conditions, pests or diseases, but weigh against these few losses the fact that organic means working with nature, not against it.

In the bigger picture, no system of farming does more to reduce greenhouse gas emissions from agriculture, or protect natural resources such as fresh water and healthy soils. Organic farms are havens for wildlife and provide homes for bees, birds and butterflies, and – most importantly here – published research points to significant differences between organic and non-organic products. Organically produced cereals, fruit and vegetables can contain more than 60 per cent more antioxidants than their non-organic counterparts, as well as lower concentrations of pesticides and toxins such as cadmium. Which would you rather cultivate, harvest – and eat?

Soaking & sprouting

When any dried seed is soaked in water, the enzymes it contains are triggered to 'come alive' and start the growth process. In nature, this activation may occur almost immediately the seed is expelled from the parent plant, or it may not happen for many years. Seeds from antiquity have been found on archaeological sites that have been successfully activated after an interval of hundreds, if not thousands, of years, allowing scientists to determine the exact nature of the contemporary vegetation.

Seeds have evolved protective compounds to ensure that they remain intact and retain their potency however they are broadcast, and whatever conditions they are subject to while they wait to start growing. Some seeds are spread by being consumed by birds and then deposited after travelling through their gut, whereas others have to survive extremes of heat or cold, or drought or flood. The protective compounds that preserve the seeds are known as phytates or phytic acid. Untreated, these can cause digestive problems for some people, but soaking your seeds will help to break down or remove the phytic acid in most seeds.

Once your seeds have rehydrated (remember chia can absorb up to 15 times its own weight in liquid), their nutrients will be far more bio-available in the gut. This means that your body will more easily be able to separate out and absorb specific nutrients including proteins, soluble and insoluble fibre, and the full array of vitamins and minerals.

Some seeds – linseeds and chia, for example – break down to create a gelatinous texture when they are soaked, which can help create mousses, jellies and other recipes that require thicker consistencies (*see* for example page 84: Chia seed porridge).

Sprouting your seeds

Choose glass jars, ceramic or china pots either with lids you can pierce, or with a ridge at the rim around which you can tie a muslin cloth (cheesecloth). This enables you to rinse the seeds with fresh water, and then tip out the excess water without losing any of the germinating seeds.

Fill your jar about one third full of seeds. Add filtered water to the brim and leave the seeds to soak overnight or for at least 12 hours to activate their enzymes. Drain fully, then refill and drain several more times with fresh water to rinse the seeds thoroughly. They will then be ready to start the sprouting process. I continue to rinse and drain my seeds every 12 hours, especially once they have started to sprout, which helps keep them as fresh as possible.

After several hours or days (depending on the size of seed and eventual plant), a tiny root starts to grow downwards, and a shoot reaches upwards towards the light and warmth. This is the first part of germination, and a process that occurs naturally in the presence of water, light and air. The 'sprouts' are the high-protein shoots. Having already absorbed the water they need, they are reaching for the sunlight to activate their chlorophyll.

Chlorophyll, which is responsible for the green pigmentation in plants, absorbs energy from the sun to facilitate photosynthesis. Chlorophyll to plants is like blood to humans, and has been shown to have antioxidant, anti-inflammatory and healing

properties when digested. It helps to alkalize the body and maintain homeostasis (cellular balance), particularly in the liver and kidneys – both organs of natural detoxification. Every sprouted seed, along with all green fruits and vegetables, is rich in alkalizing chlorophyll.

Don't forget to label your growing food. Include information such as the type of seed, when it was soaked, and when it started to sprout. Rinsing the developing sprouts thoroughly prevents bitterness, rancidity and mildew or mould spores from forming.

Some sample soaking and sprouting times are shown below, illustrating what a satisfyingly quick process it can be to produce your own living superfoods. The times and yields are guidelines only, since the exact figures will depend on the conditions you provide, and even then will vary with the prevailing temperature or available light.

SEED	QUANTITY	SOAKING TIME	SPROUTING TIME	YIELD
Sunflower	1 cup	4 hours	12–24 hours	2 cups
Pumpkin	1 cup	4 hours	12–24 hours	1¾ cups
Sesame	1 cup	4 hours	6–12 hours	1½ cups
Buckwheat	1 cup	1–4 hours	12–24 hours	2 cups
Quinoa	1 cup	3–6 hours	24 hours	3 cups

Harvesting & collecting

A plant's seeds are generally fully developed when the plant has flowered, and the flower is over, or starting to dry out. In the drying process, the seeds will fall or be blown from the plant, or released in some other way to start a new plant of their own.

Sunflowers illustrate the cycle spectacularly. Once they have flowered, they turn their heads to follow the sun throughout the daylight hours until, as the sun sets, their heads droop towards the ground, to protect the valuable seeds from any overnight chill or rain. As the sun rises the following morning, the process begins again and the sun gradually matures and dries the seed until it bursts. Sounds like distant gunshot echo around a field of mature sunflowers as the dried seeds' coating (outer skin) splits and they are released from the centre of the flower.

Commercial seed collectors use machinery to cut off the flower heads and dry them in sheds, and then to shake them on conveyor belts to remove the skins. At home, you can do this by cutting the flower head from the stalk when the seeds have changed from black to a paler green, allowing them to dry under cover wherever is convenient, then tapping the flower head over a large bowl to collect the seeds.

Pumpkin seeds, being part of the gourd family, have to be scooped out of the pumpkin when it is fully grown and ripe for cooking; then soaked in water to help release the seeds from the surrounding pithy flesh. They can then be dried gently in the oven before being ready to eat.

The much smaller coriander seeds are contained in the ovum (seed casing) that forms once the plant has flowered. This can happen more than once in a season when the seeds are grown at home, because coriander (cilantro) tends to bolt and grow too quickly if contained. To capture the fine seeds, cut the flowers as they are drying, and sit them on kitchen paper (towel) on a plate to dry completely. You can then collect the seeds by gently shaking them out of the drying fruits/flowers.

Don't let your seed run away from you

Whatever your seed, you will need to watch the plant or flowers carefully, as they can mature in a very short time, suddenly spilling their seed into the surrounding earth rather than waiting for a convenient moment for you to harvest them. Be especially vigilant in the summer when warm weather can ripen and mature the seeds during the course of a single day.

Once collected, tip a proportion of your seeds into an envelope to save for replanting next year, and the rest into airtight jars for the kitchen. There's nothing like growing seed from your own original plants for taste and nutritional value!

Drying, sourcing & storing

Drying your seed

To preserve your seeds in optimum condition, it is important to dry them before packing them away in envelopes. Ideally, they should be left out in the sun to dry, but if this is not possible or practical put them in small bowls and leave them overnight in a warm place such as near a radiator. Otherwise you could put them in a cooling oven for 10–20 minutes to dry out completely, but make sure the oven is turned off before the seeds go in, since you need only to get rid of excess moisture, not to cook them in any way.

Sourcing your seed

If you can't gather seeds that you've grown yourself and you need to buy them, it's important to do your research carefully to ensure that you find the most nutritionally-rich seeds available. Buy good-quality, original strains of organically produced seeds that have not been genetically modified. Always choose reputable companies that guarantee the source of all their seeds.

It's a good idea to check out your local organic food stores to look for really healthy, high-quality seeds. Horticultural centres such as Kew Gardens in the UK will also supply names of pure seed suppliers. The key point is not to buy mass-produced, grown-for-the-supermarkets varieties, since these could have been tainted with fertilizers and herbicides.

The store cupboard

There are many items that a good store cupboard should never be without, and a collection of well labelled and dated seeds is high on the list. However, since even dried seed can be susceptible to mould or mildew if left too long, if you are buying in large quantities they may be better stored in the freezer.

Remember to label all bought seeds with the date they were purchased so that you can easily rotate your stock. Bring frozen seeds back to room temperature before attempting to soak and sprout, or sow and grow.

Choose your containers with care. The key is to find something that will protect your seeds from heat, light, and air. A collection of ceramic or china pots with different-coloured lids or stickers could help distinguish your seeds at a glance or, if you keep your seeds in the refrigerator, you may want a collection of stacking tubs that take up minimum space and that you can label and access easily.

Avoid keeping seeds in hessian or jute bags or open containers which, although they look attractive, will not preserve the seeds in peak condition, and may attract rodents and other pests.

Roasting & toasting

I like to have my seeds available to use in fairly large quantities so that if I need only a few to sprinkle or to add to a meal for one, I don't have to think about cooking a batch specifically for the purpose. Remember that being prepared is the most efficient tool you can have in your kitchen: if you cook ahead, then store or chill the surplus seeds in the refrigerator, you can be ready at a moment's notice.

However, as with nuts, the essential fatty acids (omega nutrition) in all seeds are sensitive to heat so it is important to ensure that you don't overheat your seeds when you cook them. Different seeds should be cooked in separate batches, since some toast or roast far more quickly than others. Small seeds such as sesame can burn more easily than pumpkin or quinoa, for example.

Once you have cooked and cooled them, store them in sealed containers in the refrigerator for ultimate freshness. You can store most seeds for up to a month if chilled, so it is worth keeping a separate storage box in your refrigerator for them.

Dry-roasting

Dry-roasting, that is heating without adding oil, keeps your seeds fresh, pungent and brittle, and thus – once cooled – suitable for being ground in a pestle and mortar to elicit the best possible flavours and aromas. All the spicy seeds – coriander, cumin, fennel, caraway, nigella and mustard – are best cooked this way. It is best if you scatter them onto baking parchment on a baking (cookie) sheet and place the tray in the oven as it cools. Putting your seeds directly onto a warmed baking (cookie) sheet can cause the more delicate varieties to burn and become bitter-tasting.

Toasting or dry-frying

This method involves using a heavy-bottomed frying pan (skillet), rather than toasting in, or under, any grill (broiler). This allows you to agitate/shake the seeds in the pan to ensure an even toasting, while carefully watching the colour of your seeds. This, I have found, requires one's full attention and is not something to attempt whilst multi-tasking: something will suffer, and it's most likely to be the seeds!

Most seeds will toast fairly quickly and release their aroma as they start to heat. Using a low to medium heat allows you to preserve the essential fats. Caraway and fennel, cumin, coriander and nigella all respond well to this method. Sunflower, sesame, poppy and pumpkin seeds can also be toasted, and are then delicious added to salads, but still need to be watched carefully as they also burn easily. It is better to use chia, hemp and linseed without toasting them, however, because with very little heat these seeds can become bitter and their protein content can be damaged. These are better soaked and sprouted.

Avoid grilling (broiling) seeds, because the heat under a grill (broiler) is simply too much for the seeds and will burn them almost immediately. If you are going to add seeds to foods on a barbecue, use them (especially white and black sesame seeds) as part of a marinade where the olive oil, lemon/orange juice and other condiments partially protect the seeds from burning.

Snacks, spreads, dips & drinks

Seedy sprinkles

One of the best ways to use your seeds – especially those you have grown and harvested yourself – is to create your own sprinkles. Attractively packaged, these also make great gifts for family and friends.

Sprinkles are a wonderful way of flavouring foods, providing a great nutrition store. Remember to label and date them, and don't leave them next to your stove or other heated areas, where the essential oils in the seeds can become damaged.

Dukka sprinkle

Originating from Egypt, this heady mixture of seed-based spices combined with your choice of nuts yields one of the most delicious culinary accompaniments. Once you have made your first batch, it will become a regular favourite. A word of warning: don't get carried away – it's so moreish you may have to restrain yourself from adding it to everything.

1 tbsp almonds, skins on or off

1 tbsp pistachios, shelled

1 tbsp sesame seeds (white and/or black)

1 tsp cumin seeds

1 tsp coriander seeds

a pinch of rock salt or Himalayan pink salt

1   Using a heavy-based or non-stick frying pan (skillet), lightly toast each of the nuts and seeds separately for a few minutes until they are golden, and releasing their aromas. Shake continuously to avoid burning the seeds or damaging the delicate omega-rich oils they contain.

2   Pour the seeds and nuts into a pestle and mortar or food processor. Allow them to cool completely before adding seasoning and gently blending the ingredients. Be careful not to reduce them to powder – you still want a little crunch left in the sprinkle.

3   Store in an airtight container, or reusable jars with screw-top lids.

From left: Dukka sprinkle; Ras el hanout;
Toasty-roasty omega-seed sprinkle

Ras el hanout

Every family has its own version of this North African mixture, which is passed down through the generations. The distinctive flavour of turmeric is due to the high levels of the chemical compound curcumin it contains. Studies have suggested that curcumin has potent anti-inflammatory properties and may be particularly useful in the context of disorders such as rheumatoid arthritis.

1½ tsp coriander seeds
¾ tsp cumin seeds
½ tsp chilli seeds
1¼ tsp ground cinnamon
1 tsp paprika powder
½ tsp ground turmeric
½ tsp ground cardamom seeds
½ tsp ground ginger

1   Combine all the ingredients in a pestle and mortar and grind until the aromas are released. Add more of any of the spices you particularly favour.

2   Pack into a tightly sealed container, and date and label before storing in a cool, dark place.

Or you can try this...

❖   Mix with extra virgin olive oil to create a marinade or a dressing to rub on meat, fish and poultry.

Toasty-roasty omega-seed sprinkle

I always have a version of this at the ready to add to cereals, yoghurt, porridge, eggs, cakes, flatbreads and all manner of fish, to enhance the flavour, texture and nutritional value. Make in larger batches and freeze to prolong the life of the essential fats, whilst ensuring that you always have a ready-made stock.

2 tbsp pumpkin seeds
2 tbsp sunflower seeds
2 tbsp linseed
2 tbsp sesame seeds
a generous pinch of sea salt
½ tsp ground black pepper

1   Preheat the oven to the lowest setting.

2   Place a sheet of baking parchment on a baking (cookie) sheet and spread all the seeds evenly over the parchment.

3   Bake for no more than 10–12 minutes, shaking the tray halfway through the baking time to ensure that all the seeds are evenly cooked.

4   Turn off the oven, and leave the seeds for a further 5 minutes, before removing and pouring into a dish to cool.

5   When they're completely cooled, add seasoning to taste and transfer the sprinkle to an airtight container to store.

Seed oils & butters

There are now many ways to extract oils, some of which are used more usually with nuts, and others with seeds. With seeds, cold-pressing is the best method, as this does not damage the essential oils, or render them rancid, which other heat-based methods can. Cold-pressing does not use a centrifugal system, which tends to heat the seeds. Extra-virgin refers to the 'first pressing' of the seeds, as with olive oil, and is usually the most costly. It yields a rich, pure oil that is dense in flavour and nutrients.

Seed butters are a great source of omega-3 and omega-6 essential fatty acids, the essential fats that the body cannot manufacture by itself. Rich in vegetarian protein and B vitamins, and containing virtually no saturated fats (such as you would find in peanut butter), they are perfect spread on breads, crackers and/or with raw vegetable dippers such as carrots, celery and endive or chicory.

You may wish to toast the seeds lightly before making them into a butter or spread but again, remember to do so over a low heat, whilst constantly shaking the pan to prevent the seeds from overheating or burning. Toasting them will yield a nutty flavour. Using activated (pre-soaked) seeds (see pages 40–41) will produce a fresher, richer taste.

Pumpkin seed butter

300g/11oz/generous 2½ cups fresh pumpkin seeds, preferably pre-soaked for 4–6 hours

150ml/¼ pint/generous ½ cup extra virgin olive oil

a pinch of fennel seed

2–3 sprigs fresh thyme

juice of ½ lemon

a pinch of rock salt

1 Combine all the ingredients in a blender or food processor and blend on the lowest setting until the desired consistency is achieved.

2 Remove from blender immediately and store in an airtight container in the refrigerator.

Tahini (Sesame seed spread)

Classic tahini is usually made with toasted sesame seeds, of either the pale or white varieties. If you prefer to use toasted seeds, take care not to over-toast them, otherwise they will impart a bitter taste to the spread.

300g/11oz/2½ cups sesame seeds
125ml/4fl oz/½ cup filtered lukewarm water
3 garlic cloves, peeled
juice and zest of 1 whole unwaxed lemon
a generous pinch of sea salt
a small bunch of parsley or coriander (cilantro) leaves
olive or sesame oil to seal

1   Place all the ingredients except the herbs into a blender and blend at low speed until smooth. Serve topped with the chopped parsley or coriander (cilantro).

2   Transfer any tahini you are not going to use immediately into a screw-top jar. Pour a thin layer of olive or sesame oil over the surface to prevent the spread from oxidizing, and store in the refrigerator.

From left: Pumpkin seed butter; Sunflower seed butter; Tahini (Sesame seed spread)

Sunflower seed butter

This fresh, light and nourishing butter is similar to a smooth peanut butter in texture.

300g/11oz /2½ cups pre-soaked/activated sunflower seeds
100ml/3½fl oz/scant ½ cup organic sunflower or sesame oil
2 tbsp finely chopped chives
salt and black pepper to taste

1   Place the seeds and oil in a blender/food processor, and blend until smooth. Add the chives a little at a time, reserving a few as a garnish. Season to taste.

Serve these golden seed-studded crackers with cheese, pickles, chutneys and dips, or top them with hummus. The assorted seeds contain a plethora of nutrients and, due to the short cooking time, they are delivered with minimal damage and maximum nutrition.

Five-seed crackers

250g/9oz/generous 2½ cups plain (all-purpose) flour

1 tsp baking powder

½ tsp sea salt

75g/3oz/6 tbsp unsalted butter, diced

1 tsp nigella seeds

1 tsp caraway seeds

2 tbsp poppy seeds

1 tbsp sesame seeds

1 tbsp hemp seeds

a pinch of dried chilli flakes

freshly ground black pepper

100ml/3½fl oz/scant ½ cup iced water

1 tbsp olive oil

Makes: about 30 crackers
Prep: 20 minutes
Chill: 30 minutes
Cook: 15 minutes

TIP: *For extra crispness, when the crackers are cooked turn off the oven and open the door, leaving the crackers inside for 10 minutes to cool down gradually.*

1 Preheat the oven to 190°C, 375°F, gas mark 5. Line 2 baking (cookie) sheets with parchment paper.

2 Sift the flour and baking powder into a large bowl. Mix in the salt and rub in the butter with your fingertips until the mixture resembles fine breadcrumbs.

3 Stir in all the seeds and the chilli flakes, and add a grinding of black pepper.

4 Add the water and oil and stir with a palette knife until you have a soft dough that leaves the side of the bowl clean. Shape the dough into a ball, wrap in cling film (plastic wrap) and chill in the refrigerator for 15 minutes.

5 Cut the dough into 2 portions and roll one portion out as thinly as possible into a large rectangle on a lightly floured work surface. Cut into small neat rectangles and place on one of the lined baking (cookie) sheets. Repeat with the other portion of dough, laying out the rectangles on the second sheet.

6 Pop back into the refrigerator to chill for 15 minutes, then bake in the preheated oven for about 15 minutes until the crackers are browned and crisp.

7 Cool them on a wire rack and store in an airtight container. They will stay fresh for 4–5 days.

Or you can try this...

❖ Vary the seeds – why not try cumin, chia or pumpkin seeds, linseed or some crushed coriander seeds?

❖ Add a little finely grated Parmesan cheese or sprinkle a little over the rolled-out crackers before baking.

Serve these homemade crisp crackers with a dip or some tangy cheese and chutney. Who needs commercially produced crispbreads when these far more delicious alternatives add the nutritional benefits of several different seeds – and are so easy to make?

Seedy rye crispbreads

150g/5oz/1½ cups rye flour

100g/3½oz/1 cup wholemeal (whole-wheat) flour plus extra for dusting

½ tsp baking powder

1 tsp fine sea salt

5 tbsp olive oil

150ml/¼ pint/generous ½ cup water

80g/3oz/generous ½ cup caraway, fennel, nigella or poppy seeds (or a mixture)

Makes: 10–12
Prep: 15 minutes
Cook: 10–12 minutes

1 Preheat the oven to 200°C, 400°F, gas mark 6.

2 Put the flours, baking powder and salt in a large mixing bowl. Make a well in the middle and pour in 4 tablespoons olive oil and the water, then mix to a soft dough with a palette knife, drawing the flour in from the sides. If it's too sticky, add a little more flour; too dry, add a little more water.

3 Heat some non-stick baking (cookie) sheets in the preheated oven.

4 Knead the dough with your hands on a lightly floured board. When it's smooth, roll it out with a rolling pin, brush with the remaining olive oil and sprinkle with the seeds. Fold over and roll the seeds into the dough. Knead lightly. Divide into 10–12 pieces and roll each one to about 5mm/⅛ in thick.

5 Take the hot trays out of the oven and slide the seeded dough discs onto them. Bake in batches for 10–12 minutes until crisp.

6 Cool thoroughly on a wire rack. Store in a tin or other airtight container for up to 5 days.

Or you can try this...

❖ Add some pumpkin, chia or black or white sesame seeds to the dough.

❖ Scatter the rolled-out dough with a pinch of sea salt crystals before baking, and press them in lightly with the back of a metal spoon.

*This page: Seedy fruit and nut bars (see page 58);
opposite, above and far right: Peanut butter, sesame
and chia seed squares (see page 59)*

These crunchy bars, packed with protein and other vital nutrients, are a tasty way to sustain you when you don't have time for a sit-down meal. The relatively low oven temperature helps to preserve the essential oils in the seeds.

Seedy fruit and nut bars

1 tbsp pumpkin seeds

1 tbsp sunflower seeds

1 tbsp sesame seeds

1 tbsp linseeds

300g/11oz/3¼ cups rolled oats

80g/3oz/scant ¾ cup chopped walnuts

100g/3½oz/scant ¾ cup dried apricots, chopped

100g/3½oz/generous ½ cup stoned (pitted) Medjool dates, chopped

50g/2oz/generous ½ cup dried cranberries

50g/2oz/generous ½ cup raisins

150g/5oz/generous ½ cup butter, plus extra for greasing

6 tbsp runny honey

Makes: 12 squares
Prep: 15 minutes
Cook: 30–35 minutes

1   Preheat the oven to 170°C, 325°F, gas mark 3. Lightly butter a shallow rectangular 30 x 20cm (12 x 8in) baking tin (pan) and line with baking parchment.

2   Mix together the seeds in a small bowl.

3   Put the oats, walnuts and dried fruits in a large mixing bowl.

4   Put the butter and honey in a small frying pan (skillet) and heat gently over a low heat, stirring until the butter melts and blends with the honey. Pour over the oat mixture and stir well. Stir in the seeds until everything is thoroughly combined. If it's too dry, add a little more melted butter; too sticky, add some more oats.

5   Tip the mixture into the prepared baking tin (pan) and smooth the top, pressing down firmly with the back of a metal spoon. Bake for 30–35 minutes in the preheated oven until golden brown.

6   Remove and allow to cool slightly before cutting into squares. Leave until completely cold, then remove and store in an airtight container.

Or you can try this...

❖   Almost any nuts can be used to make these crunchy bars – chopped pecans, hazelnuts, cashews or flaked almonds all work well.

These crunchy squares make a tasty power snack at any time of day. Packed with antioxidants, zinc, selenium, and vitamins A, C and E, they are perfect for a nutritional boost on the run, or even a meal alternative. Be sure to use organic peanut butter with no added sugar.

Peanut butter, sesame and chia seed squares

125g/4oz/½ cup butter

125g/4oz/½ cup crunchy peanut butter

1 tbsp runny honey or agave syrup

2 ripe bananas, mashed

350g/12oz/3 cups porridge oats

100g/3½oz/scant ¼ cup dried apricots, chopped

25g/1oz/scant ¼ cup dried cranberries

25g/1oz/scant ¼ cup chia seeds

25g/1oz/scant ¼ cup sesame seeds

Makes: 8 bars
Prep: 10 minutes
Cook: 25–30 minutes

1　Preheat the oven to 170°C, 325°F, gas mark 3. Lightly butter a 20 x 20cm (8 x 8in) baking tin (pan) and line with baking parchment.

2　Heat the butter, peanut butter and honey or agave syrup over a low heat until the butter melts.

3　Remove from the heat, stir in the mashed bananas, oats, dried fruit and seeds until you have a sticky mixture.

4　Spoon the mixture into the prepared tin, pressing it down well with the back of a metal spoon and smoothing the top.

5　Bake in the preheated oven for 25–30 minutes until crisp and golden brown. Remove and leave to cool in the tin before cutting into squares. Store in an airtight container.

Or you can try this...

❖ Experiment with seeds such as pumpkin, sunflower, linseed and poppy.

❖ If you're feeling indulgent, add some plain (semisweet) chocolate chips, or half-dip the finished squares in melted chocolate and leave them to set.

These crisp sesame-crusted filo (phyllo) rolls with a spinach and feta filling are a variation on the traditional Greek spinach pie. Eat them as snacks, party canapés or dippers, or serve them for lunch with a salad. The sesame boosts the nutritional content, providing a hit of selenium to support the immune system.

Spanakopita rolls

2 tsp olive oil

a bunch of spring onions (scallions), thinly sliced

2 garlic cloves, crushed

350g/12oz spinach

100g/3½oz/scant ½ cup feta cheese, crumbled

a handful of dill, finely chopped

125g/4oz/15–20 sheets filo (phyllo) pastry

50g/2oz/¼ cup butter

3 tbsp white sesame seeds

salt and freshly ground black pepper

Makes: about 32
Prep: 35 minutes
Cook: 20–25 minutes

1   Preheat the oven to 180°C, 350°F, gas mark 4. Line 2 baking (cookie) sheets with baking parchment.

2   Heat the oil in a frying pan (skillet) over a low heat and gently cook the spring onions (scallions) and garlic for 4–5 minutes until tender.

3   Wash the spinach and remove any thick stalks. Shake off the water and put the leaves in a large saucepan. Place over a low to medium heat, cover the pan and cook for a few minutes, shaking occasionally, until the spinach wilts and turns bright green. Drain in a colander and use a saucer or plate to press down and squeeze out any water.

4   Chop the spinach and place in a bowl with the spring onion mixture, feta and dill. Mix together and season to taste with salt and pepper.

5   Place the sheets of filo (phyllo) pastry on a clean work surface and cut each one in half lengthways into 2 rectangles.

6   Melt the butter in a small pan over a low heat and brush lightly over a filo (phyllo) pastry rectangle. Smear a little of the spinach filling along the long side of the rectangle, leaving a small edge, and then roll up tightly. Place seam-side down on the lined baking (cookie) sheet. Repeat with the other filo (phyllo) rectangles in the same way.

7   Brush lightly with the remaining melted butter and sprinkle with sesame seeds. Bake in the preheated oven for 12–15 minutes until golden brown. The fingers are best eaten warm.

Pumpkin seed pesto

This fragrant pesto is delicious served as a dip with raw vegetables or stirred into pasta or steamed rice. Rich in omega nutrition, pumpkin seeds help to protect brain cells and support male and female hormone health.

25g/1oz/scant ¼ cup pumpkin seeds

2 tbsp pine nuts

25g/1oz/scant ¼ cup plain cashews

2 garlic cloves, crushed

80g/3oz basil, leaves and stalks

juice of 1 small lemon

125ml/4fl oz/½ cup fruity green olive oil

1 red chilli, seeded and shredded

Serves: 4
Prep: 10 minutes
Cook: 2 minutes

1   Place a dry frying pan (skillet) over a medium heat. When it's hot, add the pumpkin seeds and pine nuts. Toss gently for 2 minutes until they darken slightly. Remove from the pan.

2   Put the pumpkin seeds in a food processor or blender with the pine nuts, cashews, garlic, basil, lemon juice and most of the olive oil. Blitz to a paste. Gradually add more olive oil until you achieve the consistency you prefer: thicker for a dip; thinner for tossing with cooked pasta.

3   Stir in the chilli shreds. The pesto will keep for at least a week in an airtight container in the refrigerator.

Spiced avocado and tahini dip

Tahini is widely used for making hummus and as a flavouring or sauce in the Middle East. This delicious dip is best made by hand in a pestle and mortar to give it a chunky, coarse texture.

1 tsp cumin seeds

2 garlic cloves, chopped

a large pinch of sea salt crystals

2 ripe avocados

3 tbsp tahini

juice of 1 small lemon

2 tbsp fruity green olive oil, plus extra for drizzling

a few sprigs of coriander (cilantro), chopped

Serves: 4–6
Prep: 10 minutes
Cook: 2 minutes

1   Heat a small frying pan (skillet) over a medium heat. Add the cumin seeds to the hot pan and toast, tossing gently for 1–2 minutes until they release their aroma and have darkened slightly. Remove from the pan.

2   Crush together the garlic, sea salt and toasted cumin seeds, preferably in a large pestle and mortar.

3   Peel and stone the avocados and scoop out the flesh. Add to the pestle and mortar and mash everything together.

4   Add the tahini, lemon juice and olive oil and stir well. Stir in the coriander (cilantro).

5   Transfer to a serving bowl. Drizzle with olive oil and serve, or cover with cling film (plastic wrap) and refrigerate for an hour or two until you are ready to eat.

Top: Spiced avocado and tahini dip; centre left: Pumpkin seed pesto; right: Five-seed crackers (see page 53)

Chia and poached pear spread

Chia and poached pear spread

This is a quick and easy way to make a tasty and nutritious spread. Chia seeds' generous capacity to absorb fluid ensures that your blood-sugar levels are not adversely affected by the glucose and fructose from the poached fruit.

500g/1lb 2oz/generous 2 cups peeled, cored and chopped pears

2 tbsp lemon juice

a good pinch of ground cinnamon

a good pinch of ground nutmeg

2 tbsp runny honey or agave syrup

2 tbsp chia seeds

Makes: 1 x 350g/12oz jar
Prep: 5 minutes
Cook: 10 minutes
Stand: 1 hour

1 Put the pears, lemon juice, spices and honey or agave in a saucepan and cook gently over a low heat, stirring occasionally, for about 10 minutes until the fruit is tender and pulpy.

2 Remove from the heat and stir in the chia seeds. Mix well and set aside for 1 hour, stirring occasionally, until the mixture thickens.

3 Pour the cold mixture into a sterilized jar and store in the refrigerator. Use within 1 week. Alternatively, you can freeze the mixture for up to 3 months.

Raw chia and strawberry spread

In the summer when strawberries are cheap and plentiful, how about making them into a 'raw jam'? It's much easier and quicker than making the real thing with sugar and preserving pans. And it's healthier, too. Use as a spread or as a topping for porridge or yoghurt.

450g/1lb/generous 2½ cups strawberries, hulled

juice of 1 small lemon

2 tbsp maple syrup

2 tbsp chia seeds

Makes: 1 x 350g/12oz jar
Prep: 5 minutes
Cook: 10 minutes
Stand: 1 hour

1 Briefly blitz all but a handful of the strawberries in a blender and pour into a bowl. Chop the remaining strawberries into small pieces.

2 Stir the lemon juice and maple syrup into the strawberry purée and then mix in the chia seeds and chopped fruit.

3 Set aside in a cool place for 1 hour, stirring every 10–15 minutes, until the mixture thickens.

4 Pour into a sterilized jar and store in the refrigerator. Use within 5 days. Alternatively, you can freeze the mixture for up to 2 months.

Above: Blueberry buckwheat bliss;
left: Nectarine and cardamom smoothie

From left: Nectarine and cardamom smoothie;
Mango and chia seed breakfast smoothie;
Blueberry buckwheat bliss (see pages 68–69)

Seedy smoothies

The protein and essential fats that seeds contribute to smoothies can help to balance blood-sugar levels and provide an additional energy source as well as a delicious taste and texture. You can simply add seeds directly to your smoothies, but if you have time it's far better to soak them for at least an hour first (or even overnight, in the case of chia seeds), to activate the enzymes in the seeds. This hugely increases the accessibility of their nutrients. We recommend soaking chia seeds in batches, and storing them in the refrigerator till you need them. Seal the container or cover with cling film (plastic wrap) to prevent the seeds from absorbing scents and flavours from other foods.

Nectarine and cardamom smoothie

2 dsp sunflower seeds
2 cardamom pods
200ml/7fl oz/generous ¾ cup filtered water
80g/3oz/¾ cup ground organic almonds
2 ripe nectarines, halved and stoned (pitted)
a sprinkle of ground cinnamon (optional)

Serves: 1
Prep: 2 minutes
Stand: overnight

1   Place the sunflower seeds and cardamom pods in half the water. Place the ground almonds in the remaining water and stir. Leave both solutions to infuse/swell overnight.

2   Strain the sunflower seeds. Remove the cardamom seeds from the pods.

3   Place the sunflower and cardamom seeds, nectarines and almonds in a blender, and mix on a low setting until completely smooth.

4   Pour into a glass and sprinkle with ground cinnamon (optional).

   NOTE: *These smoothies are all fairly thick; if you prefer a thinner consistency, increase the proportion of liquid.*

Mango and chia seed breakfast smoothie

1 ripe mango, peeled and stoned (pitted)
leaves from a small sprig of fresh mint
juice of 1 lemon or lime
⅓ tsp powdered turmeric, or 1 tsp grated root turmeric
1 tbsp soaked chia seeds
150ml/¼ pint/generous ½ cup coconut milk

Serves: 1
Prep: 2 minutes
Stand: 1 hour–overnight

1   Put all the ingredients in a blender and blend at a low speed so as not to damage the delicate essential fats in the chia seeds.

2   Pour over ice, if desired, and serve straight away, or store in an airtight container.

If you have cooked buckwheat left over from supper, try mixing it into a breakfast omelette, or adding it to a smoothie to make the most of its potent proteins and minerals. To make 150g/5oz/1 cup of buckwheat, simmer 75g/2 ½oz/½ cup of groats in 300ml/½pint/1 cup of water with a pinch of ground nutmeg for 15 minutes, remove from the heat and allow to cool overnight. This smoothie also makes a great dessert.

Blueberry buckwheat bliss

200g/7oz/1 cup fresh or frozen blueberries
150g/5oz/1 cup cooked buckwheat
150ml/¼ pint/½ cup filtered water
juice of ½ lemon or lime
a pinch of Himalayan or sea salt or cracked black pepper to bring out the flavour of the blueberries

Serves: 1
Prep: 2 minutes
Stand: overnight

1 Place all the ingredients in a blender and blend at low speed, adding more filtered water if required – both the buckwheat and the blueberries have a gelatinous texture once blended.

Right: Nectarine and cardamom smoothie

Seedy tisanes

Any of these tisane recipes can be cooled, sieved and refrigerated for serving over crushed ice as a refreshing summer cocktail. Decorate with fresh sprigs of mint or ruby-red pomegranate seeds.

Fennel seed, lemon and ginger tisane

Fennel is one of the liquorice-tasting seeds and can act as a natural diuretic. This is excellent for relieving fluid retention.

1 tsp fennel seeds
½ medium unwaxed lemon, with grated zest
1cm/½in piece fresh root ginger, sliced or grated with skin on
500ml/16fl oz/2 cups boiling alkaline or filtered water

Makes: 500ml/16fl oz/2 cups

1   Place all the fennel seeds, lemon and ginger in a large porcelain or china teapot. Pour over the boiling water and cover with a lid.

2   Allow to infuse for at least 20 minutes before serving through a tea strainer.

> **CAUTION!** *You should not drink more than three cups per day if you are taking diuretic medication.*

Toasted poppy seed tisane

The poppy seeds impart a wonderful toasted nut flavour and aroma, whilst the white tea is delicate and contains immune-boosting antioxidants and polyphenols.

2–3 tsp poppy seeds
1 dsp white tea leaves
500ml/16fl oz/2 cups boiling alkaline or filtered water

Makes: 500ml/16fl oz/2 cups

1   Put the poppy seeds in a small dry frying pan (skillet) and toast until they start to pop, stirring occasionally.

2   Put the toasted seeds in a large china or earthenware teapot with the white tea leaves and pour over the boiling water. Cover with a lid.

3   Allow to infuse for at least 20 minutes before serving through a tea strainer.

Cardamom and star anise tisane

Cardamom seeds and star anise complement each other but are both quite strongly flavoured. Adjust the numbers and/or proportions to taste. This tisane is excellent for supporting the immune system.

6 cardamom seeds extracted from the pods
2 whole star anise
500ml/16fl oz/2 cups boiling alkaline or filtered water

Makes: 500ml/16fl oz/2 cups

1 Place the cardamom seeds and star anise in a large teapot. Pour over the boiling water and cover with the lid.

2 Allow to infuse for at least 20 minutes before serving through a tea strainer.

CAUTION! *This is a stimulating tisane, and should not be drunk before going to bed.*

From left: Fennel seed, lemon and ginger tisane; Toasted poppy seed tisane; Cardamom and star anise tisane

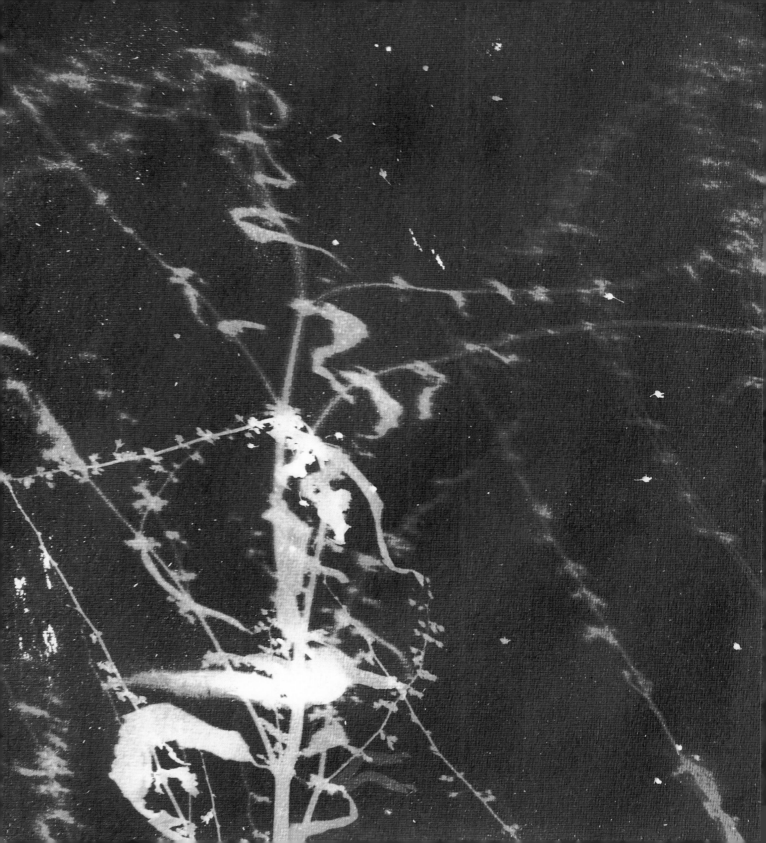

Breakfasts
& brunches

The beauty of these oat and fruit pots is that you can prepare them in minutes the night before and then enjoy them the following morning at home or 'on the go' en route to work or college. Soaking the oats overnight makes them easier to digest, breaking down the phytates that can irritate a sensitive gut – maximum nutrition with minimum effort. Nothing could be easier.

Overnight oat and fruit pots

100g/3½oz/1 cup rolled or porridge oats
250ml/8fl oz/1 cup milk
250g/8oz/1 cup low-fat plain yoghurt
1 tbsp chia seeds
1 tbsp sunflower seeds
1 tbsp pine nuts
2 tbsp chopped walnuts
2 tsp runny honey for drizzling
175g/6oz/1½ cups mixed raspberries and sliced strawberries

Serves: 2
Prep: 10 minutes
Chill: overnight

CAUTION! *Do not be tempted to use instant oats. They will break down too much and too quickly, and you will have a gooey mess with no texture.*

1 Divide the oats equally between 2 glass screw-top jars and pour the milk over them. Add the yoghurt and chia seeds and stir.

2 Mix together the sunflower seeds, pine nuts and walnuts and sprinkle over the top. Drizzle with honey.

3 Top with the mixed berries and cover each jar with a lid. Or, if you wish, add the berry topping just before eating.

4 Chill overnight in the refrigerator – preferably for 8 hours so that the oats absorb all the liquid.

Or you can try this...

❖ If you don't have any fresh fruit, you can cheat and top the oats, yoghurt, seeds and nuts with frozen fruit. They will thaw in the refrigerator overnight and the juices will percolate down into the oats.

❖ Instead of plain yoghurt, use a low-sugar fruit, vanilla or coconut variety.

❖ Flax and pumpkin seeds, and chopped pistachios can add extra crunch.

❖ For extra flavour, add a little grated lemon or orange zest or a drop or two of vanilla extract to the yoghurt and oat mixture. A pinch of salt helps, too.

Homemade granola tastes so much better than the commercial varieties, and it's healthier, too. We've served ours with tender pink rhubarb but anything goes – fresh or stewed fruit, yoghurt or plain milk. The combination of sunflower and pumpkin seeds adds substantial protein to an otherwise carbohydrate-rich breakfast cereal, providing longer-lasting energy without any spikes in blood-sugar levels.

Seedy granola bowls with pink rhubarb

450g/1lb young pink rhubarb stems, trimmed

grated zest and juice of 1 large orange

3 tbsp soft brown or Demerara sugar

1 vanilla pod (bean)

4 tbsp Greek yoghurt

milk to taste

Seedy granola:

2 tbsp coconut oil

2 tbsp honey or maple syrup

125g/4oz/1¼ cups rolled or porridge oats

2 tbsp roughly chopped hazelnuts

2 tbsp flaked almonds

25g/1oz/scant ¼ cup sunflower seeds

25g/1oz/scant ¼ cup pumpkin seeds

1 tbsp hemp seeds

a pinch of ground cinnamon

Serves: 4
Prep: 15 minutes
Cook: 35 minutes

> NOTE: *You can make the granola in advance and store it for up to a month in an airtight container.*

1 Preheat the oven to 170°C, 325°F, gas mark 3.

2 Heat the coconut oil and honey or maple syrup in a saucepan over a low heat until the coconut oil melts.

3 Add the oats, nuts, seeds and cinnamon and mix well until everything is coated. Remove from the heat.

4 Pour the granola mixture over a large baking (cookie) sheet and spread it out evenly.

5 Bake in the preheated oven for 25–30 minutes, stirring once or twice, until the granola is golden brown, crisp and toasted. Remove and leave to cool.

6 While the granola is cooking, prepare the rhubarb. Cut the stems into 2.5cm/1in pieces and arrange them in a single layer in a roasting pan. Sprinkle evenly with the grated orange zest and juice plus the brown sugar.

7 Slice the vanilla pod (bean) lengthways into halves and scrape out the seeds. Add both the empty vanilla pod (bean) and the seeds to the rhubarb.

8 Cover the rhubarb with a sheet of kitchen foil and bake in the preheated oven for about 20 minutes until tender but not mushy – it should hold its shape. Remove and set aside to cool. Discard the vanilla pod (bean).

9 Spoon the granola into 4 glass bowls or jars, add a spoonful of yoghurt and top with the cool rhubarb. Add milk if you wish.

Or you can try this...

❖ Sweeten the granola by adding dried cranberries, cherries, blueberries, sultanas (golden raisins) or diced soft ready-to-eat dried apricots.

❖ Vary the nuts in the mix, depending on what you have in the cupboard – chopped pecans and walnuts or almonds. Pine nuts also make a good addition as do coconut flakes.

These light breakfast pancakes are an American classic with a healthy seedy twist. They don't take long to prepare and cook and are perfect for a lazy weekend brunch. The seeds provide beneficial essential fatty acids as well as blood-sugar-regulating protein and fibre that will keep you going for hours!

Four-seed pancakes with avocado and roasted tomatoes

400g/14oz/2 cups cherry tomatoes, halved

1 garlic clove, crushed

2 tbsp olive oil

30g/1oz/½ cup sunflower seeds

225g/8oz/2¼ cups plain (all-purpose) flour

1 tsp baking powder

½ tsp bicarbonate of soda (baking soda)

1 tsp caster (superfine) sugar

2 large free-range eggs

300ml/½ pint/1¼ cups buttermilk

2 tbsp melted butter

2 tbsp chia seeds

1 tbsp flax seeds

1 tbsp poppy seeds

a small knob of unsalted butter for frying

2 medium avocados, halved, peeled and stoned (pitted)

maple syrup for drizzling (optional)

salt and freshly ground black pepper

Serves: 4
Prep: 15 minutes
Cook: 30 minutes

1 Preheat the oven to 200°C, 400°F, gas mark 6.

2 Place the tomatoes, cut-side up, in a roasting pan. Dot with the garlic and drizzle with the olive oil. Season with salt and pepper. Roast in the oven for 10–15 minutes.

3 Heat a dry frying pan (skillet) over a medium heat. Add the sunflower seeds in a single layer and toast for 1–2 minutes, tossing them a few times, until they are golden brown. Watch carefully that they don't catch and burn. Tip them immediately into a bowl and set aside to cool.

4 Make the pancake batter: mix the flour, baking powder, bicarbonate of soda (baking soda), sugar and a pinch of salt in a large bowl. Make a well in the centre.

5 Beat the eggs and buttermilk together in a small bowl or jug and stir in the melted butter. Pour into the flour mixture and stir well. Add all the seeds, including the toasted sunflower seeds, to the pancake batter and stir lightly again. Don't over-mix.

6 Place a large heavy-based frying pan (skillet) over a medium heat and melt a little butter in the pan. When the pan is hot, start adding the batter in tablespoons, a tablespoon at a time with space around each one, so you end up with several small pancakes per serving. Cook for about 3 minutes until they start to look dry on top and are golden brown underneath. Turn them over and cook the other side. Remove from the pan and keep warm in a low oven while you cook the remaining pancakes in the same way.

7 Mash the avocados very roughly with a fork. The flesh should still be quite lumpy.

8 Serve the hot pancakes with the smashed avocado and roasted tomatoes. Drizzle with some maple syrup if you wish.

Or you can try this...

❖ Instead of maple syrup, drizzle with a little honey and serve with some crispy bacon rashers (slices).

❖ For a more distinctive flavour and heavier texture, use half plain (all-purpose) flour and half cornmeal in the pancake batter.

Surprise seedy lemon muffins and
Seedy carrot breakfast muffins (see pages 82–83)

When you bite into these muffins, the surprise is the lemon curd that oozes out of the centre. They are delicious eaten with some fresh berries and a dollop of thick Greek yoghurt. The poppy seeds provide a burst of oleic essential fatty acid that contributes to healthy hair and skin.

Surprise seedy lemon muffins

225g/8oz/1 cup butter, softened

225g/8oz/1 cup golden caster (superfine) sugar

3 large free-range eggs

grated zest and juice of 2 lemons

250g/9oz/2½ cups plain (all-purpose) flour

3 tsp baking powder

¼ tsp salt

2 tbsp chia seeds

3 tbsp poppy seeds

3 tbsp milk

12 tsp lemon curd

Makes: 12 muffins
Prep: 15 minutes
Cook: 20–25 minutes

1 Preheat the oven to 180°C, 350°F, gas mark 4. Line a 12-hole (12-cup) muffin pan with paper cases.

2 Beat the butter and sugar in a food mixer or with an electric hand-held whisk until light and fluffy. You may need to beat for 5 minutes or so.

3 Beat in the eggs, one at a time – don't worry if the mixture curdles – and the lemon zest.

4 Sift in the flour, baking powder and salt, a little at a time, beating between each addition. Fold in the seeds and then stir in the milk and lemon juice. You should end up with a mixture that is the consistency of double (heavy) cream. If it's too stiff, add a little more milk; too runny, sift in an extra tablespoon or two of flour.

5 Divide half the mixture among the 12 paper cases, and then add a teaspoon of lemon curd to each one. Cover with the remaining mixture.

6 Bake in the preheated oven for about 20–25 minutes until well risen and golden brown. To test whether the muffins are done, insert a fine skewer into one of them – it should come out clean. Leave the muffins in the pan for a few minutes before putting them on a wire rack to cool.

7 Store the muffins in a cake tin or sealed airtight container. They will keep for 2–3 days. They also freeze well.

Or you can try this...

❖ Use grated orange zest and juice instead of lemon, and fill with orange curd.

❖ Make lemon drizzle muffins by dissolving some sugar in warm lemon juice and then brushing it over the warm cooked muffins, having pierced each one several times with a thin skewer.

❖ Dust the cooked muffins with a little icing (confectioner's) sugar.

❖ Instead of adding all the poppy seeds to the mixture, keep 1–2 teaspoons for sprinkling over the muffins before baking.

If you've never considered eating savoury muffins, now is the time to try them. The zinc and iron in the pumpkin seeds ensure enhanced energy and a healthy boost for the immune system.

Seedy carrot breakfast muffins

2 tbsp olive oil

1 red onion, diced

1 tsp ground cinnamon

¼ tsp ground nutmeg

100g/3½oz baby spinach leaves, roughly torn

2 tbsp chopped dill

250g/9oz/2½ cups self-raising (self-rising) flour

1 tsp bicarbonate of soda (baking soda)

a good pinch of salt

2 medium free-range eggs, beaten

225g/8oz/1 cup Greek yoghurt

100g/3½oz/scant 1 cup grated strong Cheddar cheese, plus extra for sprinkling

2 large carrots, grated

4 tbsp pumpkin seeds

2 tbsp pine nuts

Makes: 12 muffins
Prep: 10 minutes
Cook: 30 minutes

TIP: *These muffins freeze well so make up a batch and leave them to cool thoroughly before placing in freezer bags. They will freeze for up to a month.*

1 Preheat the oven to 200°C, 400°F, gas mark 6. Line a 12-hole (12-cup) muffin pan with paper cases.

2 Heat the olive oil in a frying pan (skillet) over a medium heat and cook the red onion for 6–8 minutes until softened. Stir in the ground spices and spinach and cook for 1 minute until the leaves turn bright green and wilt. Add the dill and set aside to cool.

3 Sift the flour, bicarbonate of soda (baking soda) and salt into a large mixing bowl.

4 Beat the eggs and yoghurt together and stir into the flour with the cooled onion and spinach mixture. Fold in the grated cheese, carrots, pumpkin seeds and pine nuts.

5 Divide the mixture between the paper cases and sprinkle lightly with the remaining grated cheese. Bake in the preheated oven for about 20 minutes until risen and golden brown. You can test whether the muffins are cooked by inserting a thin skewer into the centre – it should come out clean.

6 Leave the muffins to cool in the pan for a few minutes before transferring them to a wire rack. They are best eaten warm on the day they are made, but they will keep for a couple of days and can be reheated.

Or you can try this...

❖ Omit the spinach and add 2 coarsely grated courgettes (zucchini) with the carrots.

❖ Instead of Cheddar cheese, add some diced feta or creamy goat's cheese.

❖ Chopped walnuts, pecans, or even some thin strips of roasted red or yellow (bell) peppers make a delicious addition. For sweetness, add some grated apple. Be adventurous!

❖ Fry or grill (broil) some thin-cut bacon rashers (slices) until golden and crisp. Break into small pieces and add to the muffin mixture.

This is another really easy and healthy breakfast that can be prepared in minutes the previous evening. Overnight the chia seeds swell to thicken the almond milk, so in the morning you'll have a delicious 'porridge'. The popularity of this type of recipe has evolved through its 'quick and easy' preparation – plus chia seeds have a higher protein content than traditional oats.

Chia seed porridge

1 large banana, mashed

4 tbsp chia seeds

300ml/½ pint/1¼ cups unsweetened almond milk

grated zest of 1 orange

2 tbsp coconut yoghurt

runny honey for drizzling (optional)

Toasted nut and seed topping:

2 tbsp chopped almonds or pecans

2 tbsp flax, hemp or pumpkin seeds

2 tbsp dried cranberries

2 tbsp dried goji berries

1 tbsp coconut flakes

Serves: 2
Prep: 10 minutes
Cook: 1–2 minutes
Chill: Overnight

1 Put the mashed banana and chia seeds in a bowl and add the almond milk. Whisk well until everything is well combined, the chia seeds are distributed evenly throughout and there are no big lumps of banana.

2 Let it rest for 2–3 minutes, then whisk in the orange zest. The porridge should be starting to thicken already. Cover the bowl and leave to chill overnight in the refrigerator.

3 Heat a small dry frying pan (skillet) over a medium heat. Add the chopped nuts and seeds to the hot pan and heat, tossing them gently once or twice, for 1–2 minutes until fragrant and golden. Watch them carefully to make sure they don't burn. Remove from the pan immediately.

4 Mix the toasted nuts and seeds with the cranberries, goji berries and coconut. Set aside to cool, then transfer to a sealed container.

5 The following morning, the porridge mixture should have thickened to a tapioca-like consistency. Divide it between 2 bowls and add a spoonful of coconut yoghurt to each one. Sprinkle with the toasted nut and seed mixture. If you wish, drizzle with honey.

Or you can try this...

❖ You can use almost any combination of nuts and seeds (raw or toasted) for a topping. Try mixing with dried cherries or blueberries, raisins or diced ready-to-eat dried apricots.

❖ Fresh or poached fruit makes a good topping or accompaniment. Add some seasonal berries or fresh peaches, apricots, figs or mango. Or gently stew some sliced apple, plums or greengages with a little sugar or stevia (a natural sweetener and sugar substitute derived from the leaves of the stevia plant).

In Mexico, seeds are added to many traditional dishes. Chia seeds have long been revered in Central and South America for their energy-enhancing nutrients.

Mexican chia seed scrambled egg wraps

2 tbsp olive oil

1 small red onion, diced

1 red chilli, diced

2 tomatoes, roughly chopped

6 free-range eggs

2 tbsp chia seeds

a few sprigs of fresh coriander (cilantro), chopped

a handful of baby spinach leaves

salt and freshly ground black pepper

Wraps:

200g/7oz/generous 1½ cups self-raising (self-rising) flour

2 tbsp mixed seeds, e.g. chia, poppy, caraway, cumin

¼ tsp salt

150ml/¼ pint/generous ½ cup warm water

1½ tbsp extra virgin olive oil

Guacamole:

½ red onion, diced

1 fresh green chilli, diced

½ tsp sea salt crystals

1 garlic clove, crushed

2 ripe avocados, halved, peeled and stoned (pitted)

juice of 1 lime

a small bunch of coriander (cilantro), chopped

1 ripe tomato, seeded and diced

Serves: 2
Prep: 25 minutes
Cook: 20 minutes

1 Make the wraps: combine the flour, seeds and salt in a large bowl. Mix the warm water and oil together and add to the flour. Stir together until all the ingredients are well combined and form a dough.

2 On a floured surface, knead the dough for 2–3 minutes. Divide it into 4 balls and roll out each one individually. Aim for each tortilla to be a similar size to a dinner plate. The dough will shrink a little while it is resting.

3 In a large frying pan (skillet), warm a teaspoon of oil and cook the tortillas for 1 minute each side over a medium heat until they just start to brown on any raised areas. Keep them warm in a low oven.

4 Make the guacamole: crush the red onion, chilli and garlic in a pestle and mortar. Mash the avocado flesh roughly with a fork and stir in the lime juice. Add the coriander (cilantro), crushed onion mixture and tomato and mix well. Season with salt and pepper.

5 Heat the olive oil in a non-stick frying pan (skillet) and cook the red onion and chilli over a medium heat for 8–10 minutes until tender. Add the tomatoes and cook for 2–3 minutes.

6 Meanwhile, beat the eggs with the chia seeds and coriander (cilantro). Season lightly with salt and pepper.

7 Pour the egg mixture into the pan and stir with a wooden spoon until the eggs start to scramble and set.

8 Spread each warm tortilla with guacamole and scatter with spinach. Pile the scrambled egg mixture on top and roll up tightly or fold over to make a parcel. Serve immediately.

Or you can try this...

❖ If you love hot spicy flavours, drizzle some fiery hot chilli sauce over the filling before rolling up the wraps, or add more chilli to the guacamole or red onion mixture. Jalapeños will yield moderate heat but Scotch bonnets will turn it up to an intense level!

You can eat this versatile dish warm for breakfast, brunch or supper, or cold as a packed lunch. To make it more economical, choose smoked salmon trimmings instead of buying whole slices to cut up. The fennel seeds add a delicious aniseed flavour.

Smoked salmon tortilla with fennel seed and sofrito

2 tbsp olive oil

1 red onion, finely chopped

1 garlic clove, crushed

1 medium carrot, diced

2 celery sticks, diced

2 tbsp fennel seeds

8 organic medium eggs

a small bunch of dill, chopped

200g/7oz smoked salmon, cut into thin strips

salt and freshly ground black pepper

Serves: 4
Prep: 10 minutes
Cook: 20–25 minutes
Stand: 5 minutes

1 Make the sofrito: heat the oil in a large non-stick frying pan (skillet) over a low to medium heat. Cook the onion, garlic, carrot and celery, stirring occasionally, for about 5 minutes until tender. Stir in the fennel seeds.

2 In a clean bowl, beat the eggs until foamy and stir in the dill, smoked salmon and some salt and pepper.

3 Pour the egg mixture into the pan and stir into the sofrito. Reduce the heat as low as it can go and cook gently for 10–15 minutes until it is set and golden underneath, and the top is beginning to set.

4 Meanwhile, preheat a grill (broiler) until it's really hot. Put the pan under the grill for a few minutes until the top is set, puffy and appetizingly golden.

5 Slide the tortilla out of the pan onto a plate or board. Leave to cool for 5 minutes, then cut into wedges. Serve lukewarm with salad.

Or you can try this...

❖ For a vegetarian option, use 400g/14oz cooked, diced potatoes with the sofrito instead of the salmon.

❖ For a richer, creamier flavour, add a couple of spoonfuls of mascarpone with the egg mixture.

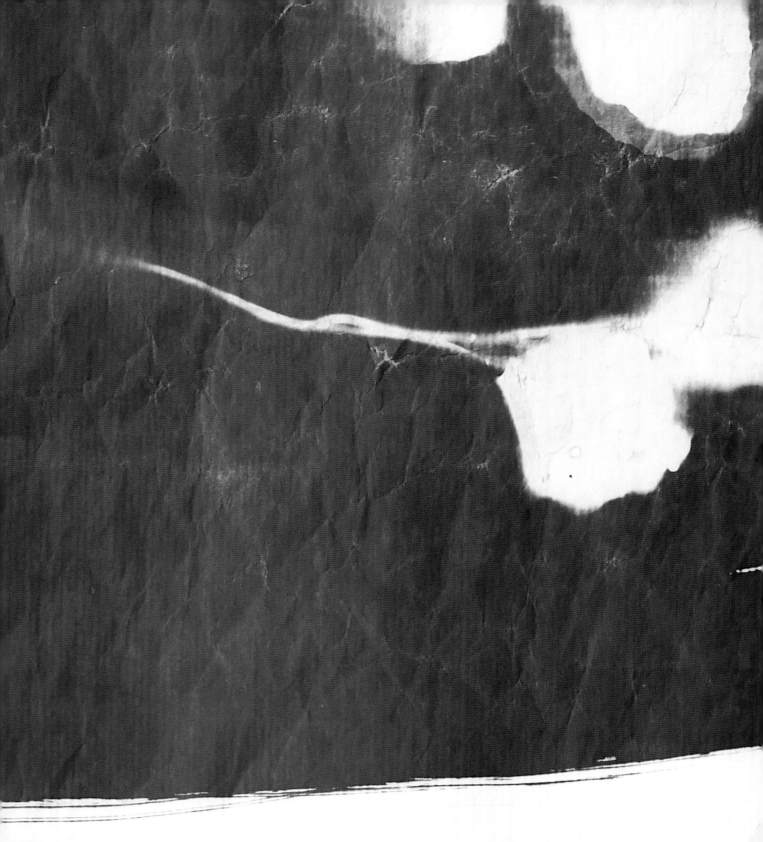

Salads & raw dishes

Tabbouleh is traditionally made with bulghur wheat, but quinoa works well, too. Cooking it in vegetable stock instead of water adds depth of flavour. Known as the 'king of seeds' in the superfood world, pomegranate seeds provide abundant vitamin C for boosting immunity and contributing to the collagen matrix of the skin – a nourishing face pack on a plate!

Green quinoa tabbouleh with pomegranate seeds

150g/5oz/scant 1 cup quinoa

400ml/14fl oz/1¾ cups vegetable stock

60g/2oz/scant ½ cup shelled pistachios

100g/3½oz curly kale, roughly chopped

100g/3½oz baby spinach leaves, shredded

60g/2oz wild rocket (arugula), roughly chopped

a bunch of spring onions (scallions), chopped

¼ cucumber, diced

a small bunch of mint, chopped

1 avocado, peeled, stoned (pitted) and cubed

2 tbsp pine nuts

1 tsp ground allspice

seeds of 1 pomegranate

Lemony sesame dressing:

1 green bird's eye chilli, finely chopped

1 garlic clove, crushed

2 tsp white sesame seeds

¼ tsp sea salt crystals

4 tbsp fruity olive oil

juice of 1 lemon

Serves: 4
Prep: 20 minutes
Cook: 15 minutes

1 Rinse the quinoa in a sieve under a cold running tap. Bring the vegetable stock to the boil in a large saucepan and add the quinoa. Reduce the heat, cover the pan and simmer for 12–15 minutes until just tender. Turn off the heat and leave to steam in the pan for 5 minutes. Drain well, fluff up with a fork and set aside to cool.

2 Heat a non-stick frying pan (skillet) over a medium heat. Add the pistachios to the hot pan and toast, tossing gently, for 1–2 minutes until fragrant and golden. Watch them carefully to ensure they don't burn. Tip them out of the pan and cool a little before chopping roughly.

3 Make the dressing: in a pestle and mortar crush the chilli, garlic, sesame seeds and sea salt crystals. Gradually add the oil, stirring it into the garlicky paste, and then stir in the lemon juice. You should end up with a well amalgamated dressing.

4 Put the kale, spinach, rocket (arugula), spring onions (scallions), cucumber and mint in a large bowl. Mix well. Add the avocado and pine nuts, and sprinkle over the allspice. Gently stir in the cooled pistachios and quinoa.

5 Toss everything lightly together in the dressing and then divide the tabbouleh between 4 serving plates. Scatter the pomegranate seeds over the top and serve.

Or you can try this...

❖ Instead of rocket (arugula) or spinach, add some peppery watercress to the tabbouleh.

❖ For a different aromatic flavour and fragrance, leave out the mint and use the same quantity of fresh coriander (cilantro).

❖ You can make this delicious dish even more seedy by adding a teaspoon of nigella seeds to the cooked quinoa.

Turn a traditional Lebanese salad into something special by making the flatbreads yourself – it's easier than you think. Warm flatbreads make a great snack spread with hummus or a seed butter. Both cumin and coriander seeds provide the palmitic and oleic essential fatty acids that are so important for hormone balance and brain function, as well as antioxidants that have anti-inflammatory properties.

Fattoush with seedy flatbreads

300g/11oz/1½ cups baby plum tomatoes, halved

6 spring onions (scallions), finely sliced

½ cucumber, diced

a bunch of radishes, trimmed and thinly sliced

2 baby gem lettuces, shredded

a bunch of mint, chopped

a bunch of flat-leaf parsley, chopped

seeds of ½ pomegranate (optional)

Sumac dressing:

grated zest and juice of 1 lemon

5 tbsp fruity olive oil

1 garlic clove, crushed

1 tbsp sumac

salt and freshly ground black pepper

Seedy flatbreads:

200g/7oz/scant 2 cups strong bread flour plus extra for dusting

½ tsp coarse sea salt crystals

1 tbsp cumin seeds, crushed

1 tbsp coriander seeds, crushed

125ml/4fl oz/generous ½ cup lukewarm water

1 tsp caster (superfine) sugar

5g sachet/scant ½ oz fast-action yeast

1 tbsp olive oil plus extra for brushing

Serves: 4
Prep 45 minutes
Rise: 90 minutes
Cook: 12–16 minutes

1 Make the flatbreads: mix together the flour, salt and seeds in a large bowl and make a well in the centre. In another smaller bowl, whisk the water, sugar and yeast. Set aside for 10–15 minutes until the mixture starts to froth.

2 Add the yeast mixture and olive oil to the flour and mix with your hands until you have a soft, sticky mixture. Turn out the dough onto a lightly floured clean surface and knead until it's elastic, smooth and firm. Place in a clean oiled bowl and cover with a cloth. Set aside in a warm place for about 90 minutes until the dough doubles in size.

3 Knock down the dough – put it on a lightly floured surface and fold it repeatedly in on itself using the heels of your hands until it is smooth and all the air is 'knocked' out of it – and then knead briefly on a lightly floured surface before dividing it into 8 equal-sized pieces. Roll each one out into an oval about 3mm/⅛ in thick. Brush them lightly with olive oil.

4 Place a large griddle pan over a medium heat and cook the flatbreads, in batches, for 3–4 minutes until golden brown underneath, then flip them over and cook the other side. Remove from the pan and cool on a wire rack.

5 Make the dressing: whisk all the ingredients together in a small bowl or shake well in a screw-top jar until well amalgamated.

6 Place all the salad vegetables and herbs in a large serving bowl and mix together.

7 Toast 4 flatbreads until crisp, then break them into small bite-sized pieces. Add them to the salad and toss everything lightly in the dressing. Check the seasoning, sprinkle with pomegranate seeds (if using) and serve with the remaining flatbreads.

Or you can try this...

❖ Add some diced green, or even some grilled (broiled) red or yellow (bell) pepper strips to the salad.

❖ Try adding some fennel seeds to the flatbread dough or some dried chilli flakes.

It doesn't take long to make a delicious hummus if you cheat and use canned chickpeas. This dish is a great way of increasing your fibre intake to help transport food through the digestive tract.

Beetroot and coriander seed hummus salad

400g/14oz pumpkin, seeded, rind removed, and cut into wedges

400g/14oz golden or red beetroot (beets), washed and cut into wedges

3 tbsp olive oil plus extra for drizzling

a good pinch of ground cinnamon

1 tsp crushed coriander seeds

80g/3oz mixed baby spinach leaves, rocket (arugula) and watercress

125g/4oz/1 cup diced feta cheese

1 tbsp red wine vinegar

juice of 1 orange

a pinch of paprika or za'atar

salt and freshly ground black pepper

Mixed seeds sprinkle:

2 tbsp pumpkin seeds

2 tbsp sunflower seeds

1 tsp black sesame seeds

Coriander seed hummus:

1 x 400g/14oz can chickpeas

100g/3½oz/scant ½ cup tahini

2 garlic cloves, crushed

2 tsp crushed coriander seeds

juice of 1 lemon

a few sprigs of coriander (cilantro)

Serves: 4
Prep: 20 minutes
Cook: 30 minutes

1   Preheat the oven to 200°C, 400°F, gas mark 6.

2   Arrange the pumpkin and beetroot (beets) on a baking (cookie) sheet and drizzle with olive oil. Dust with the cinnamon and sprinkle the coriander seeds over the top. Season with salt and pepper. Roast in the preheated oven for 25–30 minutes or until the vegetables are tender.

3   Meanwhile, make the hummus: drain the chickpeas, reserving some of the liquid. Put them in a food processor with the tahini, garlic, coriander seeds, lemon juice and coriander (cilantro). Pulse to a thick purée. It shouldn't be too smooth or creamy. If it's too thick, thin with a little of the reserved chickpea liquid. Transfer to a bowl and set aside.

4   Heat a large frying pan (skillet) and place over a medium heat. Add the pumpkin and sunflower seeds, spreading them out well, and toast for 1–2 minutes, turning and tossing them gently until golden brown. Take care that they do not burn. Remove immediately and mix with the sesame seeds.

5   Put the salad leaves, roasted vegetables and feta in a large dish. Whisk the olive oil, vinegar and orange juice together and use to dress the salad.

6   Serve with the hummus, dusted with paprika or za'atar and sprinkled with toasted seeds all over the top.

Or you can try this...

❖   Use butternut squash or sweet potato instead of pumpkin. Roast some red onion wedges or aubergine (eggplant) at the same time.

❖   Make the hummus more creamy by folding in some 0% fat Greek yoghurt to the desired consistency.

This versatile salad can be easily transformed from an appetizer or light lunch into a main meal. Make good use of the attractive feathery tops from the fennel bulbs: snip them over the salad just before serving.

Fennel and hummus salad with pomegranate seeds

2 fennel bulbs, trimmed and thinly sliced

1 tbsp fruity green olive oil

400g/14oz cooked small golden beetroot (beets), sliced

a bunch of spring onions (scallions), thinly sliced

125g/4oz/2 cups mixed sprouted seeds, e.g. alfalfa, broccoli

1 handful of mint, chopped

1 handful of flat-leaf parsley, chopped

225g/8oz/2 cups diced feta

3–4 tbsp orange and lemon poppy seed dressing (*see page 121*)

1 quantity coriander seed hummus (*see page 97*)

½ tsp za'atar

seeds of 1 pomegranate

salt and freshly ground black pepper

Serves: 4
Prep: 15 minutes
Cook: 6 minutes

1 Drizzle the fennel slices with the olive oil and cook on a hot griddle pan over a high heat or a barbecue for about 3 minutes each side until they are slightly tender and lightly charred.

2 Put the fennel in a bowl with the beetroot (beets), spring onions (scallions), sprouted seeds, herbs and feta. Season with a little salt and pepper, add the dressing, and toss.

3 Take 4 serving plates and smear the hummus generously in a circle on each one.

4 Top with the fennel and feta mixture. Sprinkle with za'atar and pomegranate seeds and serve while the fennel is still warm.

Or you can try this...

❖ Use griddled sliced halloumi cheese instead of feta or, for a more substantial dish, mix with some quinoa or sprouted buckwheat.

❖ Mix in some sliced oranges or peaches for a sweeter, more refreshing salad.

You can use any sprouted seeds in this nutritious salad. Red amaranth sprouts look sensational: the tiny seeds are fast to germinate and easy to sprout at home. Rich in vegetarian protein, this salad makes a great packed lunch to take to work or college, as the sprouting continues until the seeds are refrigerated or frozen, providing you with abundant energy.

Superfood mixed sprouts and seedy salad

225g/8oz kale, trimmed and cut into pieces

2 tbsp pumpkin seeds

80g/3oz/generous ½ cup hazelnuts

1 courgette (zucchini), cut into matchsticks

2 carrots, coarsely grated or cut into thin strips with a potato peeler

2 spring onions (scallions), sliced

150g/5oz/2 cups edamame beans, cooked or frozen and defrosted

150g/5oz/2¼ cups mixed sprouted seeds, e.g. amaranth, bean, alfalfa, broccoli, radish, peas

a small bunch of flat-leaf parsley, chopped

100g/3½oz/1 cup diced blue cheese, e.g. Roquefort or Gorgonzola

Seedy orange dressing:

4 tbsp olive oil

2 tbsp cider vinegar

1 tbsp grated ginger

1 garlic clove, crushed

grated zest and juice of 1 orange

1 tsp runny honey or pomegranate molasses

2 tbsp white sesame seeds

salt and freshly ground black pepper

Serves: 4
Prep: 15 minutes
Cook: 2 minutes

1   Blanch the kale by adding it to a saucepan of boiling salted water. Cook for 30 seconds and then drain well in a colander.

2   Toast the pumpkin seeds and hazelnuts in a dry frying pan (skillet) set over a medium heat for 1–2 minutes, tossing gently, until golden brown. Remove from the heat and set aside to cool.

3   Put the courgette (zucchini), carrots, spring onions (scallions), edamame beans, sprouts and warm kale in a large bowl. Add the parsley and toasted seeds.

4   Whisk together all the ingredients for the dressing until thoroughly combined, and pour over the salad. Add the crumbled blue cheese and toss everything gently together. Serve immediately.

Or you can try this...

❖   Instead of kale you can use raw rocket (arugula), spinach, watercress or pea shoots. For a crunchier texture, add some thinly sliced fennel bulb.

❖   Walnuts, pecans, cashews, pistachios or flaked almonds can be substituted for the hazelnuts.

❖   To make the salad more substantial, mix in some cooked quinoa or buckwheat.

An excellent source of vitamins and minerals, cauliflower is also a good choice if you want to reduce your intake of carbs. Cauliflower 'rice' is so easy to make: just blitz in a food processor and then warm through in a little flavoured oil. Make this a filling supper dish by adding beans or chickpeas, griddled halloumi, tofu or chicken. The tiny black mustard seeds provide abundant selenium, which helps to regulate the metabolism and support immunity.

Seedy cauliflower 'rice' salad with roasted pumpkin

450g/1lb peeled pumpkin, seeded and cut into large cubes

2 red onions, cut into wedges

4 tbsp olive oil

3 tbsp pumpkin seeds

1 large cauliflower

2 garlic cloves, crushed

1 tbsp black mustard seeds

a pinch of hot dried chilli flakes

60g/2oz wild rocket (arugula)

60g/2oz sun-blush tomatoes, chopped

a handful of coriander (cilantro), chopped

juice of 1 lemon

salt and freshly ground black pepper

Serves: 4
Prep: 15 minutes
Cook: 35 minutes

1 Preheat the oven to 180°C, 350°F, gas mark 4.

2 Arrange the pumpkin and red onions on a large baking (cookie) sheet and drizzle with 3 tablespoons olive oil. Grind some salt and pepper over them and roast in the preheated oven for 25–30 minutes until tender.

3 Heat a dry frying pan (skillet) over a medium heat and add the pumpkin seeds to the hot pan. Toast for 1–2 minutes, tossing them gently, until golden. Remove immediately and set aside.

4 Cut the cauliflower in half and discard the central core. Chop into small pieces. Put the pieces in a food processor and pulse them several times until they have the consistency of grains of rice.

5 Heat the remaining oil in a large frying pan (skillet) over a low to medium heat and cook the garlic and mustard seeds for 2 minutes. Add the chilli flakes and cauliflower and cook for 3–5 minutes, stirring well, until the cauliflower is warm and crunchy.

6 Tip into a large serving bowl with the rocket (arugula), sunblush tomatoes and coriander (cilantro). Add the roasted vegetables and toasted pumpkin seeds and toss gently. Drizzle with lemon juice and season to taste.

Or you can try this...

❖ Instead of coriander (cilantro), which has a very distinctive flavour, use mint or flat-leaf parsley.

❖ Try adding some sultanas (golden raisins), pine nuts, preserved lemon, sumac, cumin seeds and thick yoghurt for a Middle Eastern twist.

Make the most of new seasonal spring vegetables by eating them raw in a healthy, refreshing coleslaw. This will spring-clean your body. The essential fats in nigella, mustard and fennel seeds are beneficial for weight management, heart and brain health.

Spring coleslaw with grapefruit and mixed seeds

½ small white cabbage, cored and shredded

a head of spring greens, shredded

a bunch of spring onions (scallions), finely chopped

1 fennel bulb, trimmed and thinly sliced

1 tbsp fennel seeds

1 tbsp black mustard seeds

1 tbsp nigella seeds

1 tbsp pine nuts

2 ruby red grapefruit

3 tbsp fruity green olive oil

1 tbsp cider vinegar

a handful of mint, chopped

a few basil leaves, torn

Serves: 4
Prep: 15 minutes
Cook: 2 minutes

1 Put the cabbage, spring greens, spring onions (scallions) and fennel in a large bowl.

2 Toast the seeds and pine nuts, tossing them gently in a frying pan (skillet) for 1–2 minutes over a medium heat until they release their aroma. Do not allow them to burn. Remove from the pan and set aside to cool.

3 Cut the peel and white pith off 1 grapefruit. Cut between the membranes to release the juicy segments and add them to the vegetables.

4 Squeeze the juice of the remaining grapefruit into a small bowl and whisk in the olive oil and cider vinegar. Pour over the salad and toss gently with the toasted seeds, mint and basil.

Or you can try this...

❖ Instead of a fresh citrusy dressing, mix together some good mayonnaise with a little creamed horseradish. Thin it down with some low-fat natural yoghurt.

❖ If the dressing is too sharp for your taste, add a teaspoon of runny honey.

❖ Shave some tender raw asparagus stems into the coleslaw or add thinly sliced sugar-snap peas, some pea shoots or rocket (arugula).

This spicy coleslaw in a creamy dressing is very versatile. Serve it with cold ham or grilled (broiled) chicken, sausages or even leftover turkey. It also makes a great topping for baked jacket potatoes. Fenugreek seeds are a rich source of the entire group of B vitamins, needed for energy production and folate, which is essential in pregnancy. In conjunction with black mustard and cumin, fenugreek supports the immune system.

Winter coleslaw with fenugreek, mustard and cumin seeds

60g/2oz/scant ½ cup shelled pistachio nuts

1 small red cabbage, cored and finely shredded

1 red onion, thinly sliced

2 carrots, coarsely grated

6 Medjool dates, chopped

a handful of flat-leaf parsley, chopped

a handful of coriander (cilantro), chopped

juice of 1 orange

a large pinch of ground cinnamon

Seedy yoghurt dressing:

2 tbsp olive oil

2 red chillies, seeded and diced

2.5cm/1in piece fresh root ginger, peeled and diced

1 tsp cumin seeds

1 tsp black mustard seeds

¼ tsp fenugreek seeds

150g/5oz/generous ½ cup 0% fat Greek yoghurt

salt and freshly ground black pepper

Serves: 4–6
Prep: 20 minutes
Cook: 5 minutes

1 Place a small frying pan (skillet) over a medium heat and toast the pistachios for 1–2 minutes, tossing gently, until golden brown. Remove from the pan immediately and set aside to cool.

2 Put the red cabbage, red onion, carrots, dates and herbs in a large serving bowl. Sprinkle with the orange juice and cinnamon.

3 Make the dressing: gently cook the chillies and ginger for 2–3 minutes in the oil over a low heat. Add the seeds and cook for 1–2 minutes until they release their aroma. Remove from the heat and stir in the yoghurt. Season to taste with salt and pepper.

4 Pour the dressing over the salad and toss gently until everything is lightly coated. Sprinkle with the toasted pistachios and serve.

Or you can try this...

❖ Add the chopped segments of a peeled juicy orange or some seasonal clementines, or some diced mango. As a colourful finishing touch, sprinkle the coleslaw with ruby-red pomegranate seeds.

❖ Use lemon instead of orange juice for a sharper flavour.

The distinctive nutty and earthy flavour of buckwheat adds intensity to this colourful salad. And the B vitamins it contains contribute to energy production at a cellular level, giving you all-day energy.

Buckwheat, broccoli and sprouted seed salad

100g/3½oz/scant ¾ cup roasted buckwheat (*kasha*)

400g/14oz tenderstem broccoli, trimmed and each stalk cut in half

2 tbsp sunflower seeds

2 tbsp sesame seeds

80g/3oz sun-blush tomatoes in olive oil

125g/4oz/2 cups mixed sprouted seeds, e.g. alfalfa, broccoli, radish

1 avocado, peeled, stoned (pitted) and thinly sliced

1 quantity toasted sesame honey vinaigrette (*see* page 121)

150g/5oz soft creamy goat's cheese, cut into pieces

a pinch of dried chilli flakes

a small bunch of chives, snipped

salt and freshly ground black pepper

Serves: 4
Prep: 15 minutes
Cook: 10 minutes

1 Cook the buckwheat: put 150ml/¼ pint/generous ½ cup cold water in a small saucepan and bring to the boil. Reduce the heat to a bare simmer and add the buckwheat. Stir, then cover the pan and cook gently for about 6–8 minutes, stirring occasionally, until the buckwheat is just tender, not mushy. Take care that you do not overcook it. Leave to stand, covered, for 2–3 minutes, then spread it out on a large plate or baking (cookie) sheet and set aside to cool.

2 Steam the broccoli in a steamer or a colander placed over a saucepan of simmering water for about 5 minutes until it is just tender but still a little crisp with some 'bite'.

3 Toast the sunflower and sesame seeds in a frying pan (skillet) set over a medium heat for 1–2 minutes, tossing them gently, until golden brown. Remove and cool.

4 Drain the sun-blush tomatoes and cut them into small pieces. Mix with the sprouted seeds, avocado, buckwheat and warm broccoli in a large bowl. Toss gently in the dressing and season to taste with salt and pepper.

5 Divide the salad between 4 serving plates and dot with the goat's cheese. Sprinkle with the chilli flakes, chives and toasted seeds and serve.

Or you can try this...

❖ Add some baby spinach leaves or rocket (arugula) to the salad.

❖ Use toasted pumpkin or fennel seeds and try a different dressing – the chilli, lemon and coriander seed dressing works well (*see* page 120), especially if you add some chopped fresh coriander (cilantro) to the salad.

There's a seed jackpot in this jewelled couscous, even the prawns (shrimp) being coated with crushed seeds. It's a perfect example of how adding seeds to a grain dish can go a long way towards balancing its protein/carbohydrate content. The fibre helps to balance blood-sugar levels in the body, reducing the need for snacking throughout the day.

Jewelled couscous with spicy shrimp

175g/6oz/1 cup couscous

350ml/12fl oz/1½ cups hot vegetable stock

3 tbsp olive oil

80g/3oz/½ cup cashews

60g/2oz/scant ½ cup sultanas (golden raisins)

400g/14oz raw peeled tiger prawns (shrimp)

3 tbsp pumpkin seeds

a handful of parsley, chopped

a bunch of mint, chopped

juice of 2 limes

seeds of 1 pomegranate

harissa to serve (optional)

labneh to serve (optional)

salt and freshly ground black pepper

Spicy paste:

1 tsp coriander seeds

1 tsp cumin seeds

2 garlic cloves

1 red chilli, chopped

2–3 tbsp Greek yoghurt

Serves: 4
Prep: 20 minutes
Soak: 15 minutes
Cook: 5 minutes

1   Put the couscous in a large bowl and pour over the vegetable stock. Add the olive oil and then cover the bowl and set aside for about 12–15 minutes until the couscous grains swell and absorb the liquid.

2   Meanwhile, toast the cashew nuts lightly by tossing them in a dry frying pan (skillet) over a medium heat for 2 minutes until they are golden brown. Remove from the pan.

3   Put the sultanas (golden raisins) in a bowl and pour some boiling water over them. Leave to soak for 5–10 minutes until plump and softened. Drain well.

4   Make the spicy paste: grind the coriander and cumin seeds with a pestle and mortar. Add the garlic and chilli and keep grinding and crushing until you have a paste. Transfer to a bowl and stir in the yoghurt. Add the prawns (shrimp) and coat them lightly with the mixture. If you wish, you can do this in advance and leave them to marinate for a few hours in the refrigerator.

5   Gently mix the cashews, sultanas (golden raisins), pumpkin seeds and most of the herbs (reserving some for the garnish) into the couscous to distribute them evenly throughout. Stir in the lime juice and pomegranate seeds and season to taste with salt and pepper.

6   Heat a non-stick griddle pan over a medium heat, and when it's really hot add the prawns (shrimp). Cook quickly for 2 minutes each side until they turn pink and are cooked through. Don't overcook them or they will lose their juicy succulence.

7   Divide the couscous between 4 serving plates and pile the griddled prawns (shrimp) on top. Sprinkle with the remaining chopped parsley and mint and serve immediately with a dash of fiery harissa, if wished. Labneh also makes a good accompaniment.

Or you can try this...

❖   Vegetarians can top the couscous with grilled (broiled) halloumi or tofu, or scatter over some crumbled cheese.

❖   Instead of prawns (shrimp), serve with griddled sliced chicken or lean lamb fillet. You can coat it in the same spicy paste.

Fresh-looking green sprouted seeds and black sesame seeds look best in this salad, which balances protein, carbs, vitamins and minerals in a delicious and unusual way. You can buy toasted sesame oil in most supermarkets – it is darker, more intensely flavoured and more aromatic than regular sesame oil.

Japanese-style brown rice salad with griddled tuna

225g/8oz/1 cup brown rice

125g/4oz/generous 1½ cups frozen edamame beans

150g/5oz/2¼ cups sprouted seeds, e.g. mizuna, mung, radish

4 spring onions (scallions), sliced diagonally

olive oil for brushing or spraying

4 x 100g/3½oz tuna steaks

1 sheet ready-toasted sushi nori, cut into thin shreds

2 tbsp toasted black or white sesame seeds

Dressing:

2 tbsp sunflower oil

2 tbsp toasted sesame oil

1 tbsp miso paste

1 tbsp rice vinegar

1 tbsp mirin

juice of ½ lime

1 garlic clove, crushed

2 tsp grated fresh root ginger

1 tsp runny honey

Serves: 4
Prep: 15 minutes
Cook: 20 minutes

1   Cook the brown rice according to the instructions on the packet. Remove from the pan and leave to cool in a large bowl.

2   Add the beans to a pan of boiling water and cook for 3 minutes. Drain and refresh under running cold water. Drain and set aside.

3   Make the dressing: whisk all the ingredients together until well blended. Alternatively, place them in a screw-top jar and shake vigorously.

4   Gently stir the rice with a fork to break up any clumps and separate the grains. Mix in the edamame beans, sprouted seeds and spring onions (scallions). Pour most of the dressing over the top and toss gently together.

5   Lightly brush or spray a non-stick griddle pan with oil and place over a medium to high heat. Add the tuna steaks to the hot pan and cook for 2–3 minutes on each side, depending on how well cooked you like them. Cut each steak into slices.

6   Divide the rice salad between 4 serving plates. Top each one with the sliced tuna and drizzle with the remaining dressing. Sprinkle with the shredded nori and sesame seeds and serve immediately. Steamed tenderstem broccoli or fine green beans go well with this dish.

Or you can try this...

❖   Coat the tuna steaks in sesame seeds before frying them in a little mixed sesame and sunflower oil.

❖   Instead of tuna, top the brown rice with sliced griddled chicken or tofu.

❖   To vary the rice salad, add some sliced avocado, radishes, red or yellow (bell) peppers, cooked soya beans or chopped coriander (cilantro).

There's a seed bonanza in this warm vibrant salad, which is especially good when you want to eat something refreshing and light on cold winter days. The dark-green leafy kale is loaded with nutrients, especially antioxidants that counter free radical damage.

Roasted kale and carrot salad with crispy prosciutto

3 carrots, peeled and cut into chunky matchsticks

3 tbsp olive oil

1 tsp crushed coriander seeds

60g/2oz/scant ½ cup mixed sunflower and flax seeds

300g/11oz kale, stalks removed and roughly shredded

8 wafer-thin slices Parma ham

100g/3½oz Taleggio, rind removed and cut into pieces

2 pears, peeled, cored and sliced

4 tsp balsamic vinegar

1 tbsp black sesame seeds

salt and freshly ground black pepper

Serves: 4
Prep: 10 minutes
Cook: 20–22 minutes

1 Preheat the oven to 190°C, 375°F, gas mark 5.

2 Put the carrots in a large roasting pan and sprinkle over the oil and coriander seeds. Season lightly with salt and pepper.

3 Bake in the preheated oven for 6–8 minutes and then sprinkle the mixed seeds over the top and roast in the oven for 4 minutes.

4 Add the kale and stir everything well to turn the vegetables in the seedy oil. Return to the oven for 10 minutes until the carrots are tender and the kale is crisp.

5 Meanwhile, heat a large frying pan (skillet) over a medium heat. When it's really hot, add the Parma ham to the dry pan and cook for 1–2 minutes until crisp and golden brown. Remove immediately and drain on kitchen paper (towel).

6 Mix the warm roasted vegetables with the Taleggio pieces and divide between 4 serving plates. Add the sliced pears and the ham, and drizzle with balsamic vinegar. Sprinkle with black sesame seeds and serve warm.

Or you can try this...

❖ For a spicier flavour, use cumin instead of coriander seeds. And add some grated lemon zest and diced red chilli or dried chilli flakes with the kale.

❖ Garlic-lovers can crush 1–2 cloves and tuck them between the carrots.

This bright, zingy and refreshing salad is a great way to use up leftover cooked chicken or turkey. It tastes good at any time of the year and combines toasted and sprouted seeds to maximum effect, in terms of both nutrition and flavour.

Szechuan bang bang chicken salad with toasted sesame seeds

100g/3½oz pak choi (bok choy) leaves, sliced

2 carrots, cut into thin strips with a potato peeler or shredded

½ cucumber, halved, seeded and cut into thin strips or shredded

4 spring onions (scallions), cut into thin strips, plus extra to garnish

150g/5oz/2¼ cups sprouted seeds, e.g. mung beans, broccoli, alfalfa, sunflower

a small bunch of coriander (cilantro), chopped

450g/1lb cooked chicken breasts, skinned and shredded

1 red chilli, seeded and shredded (optional)

2 tbsp toasted white sesame seeds

lime wedges, to garnish

Bang bang dressing:

100g/3½oz/scant ½ cup crunchy peanut butter

1 mild red chilli, seeded and diced

1 garlic clove, crushed

½ tsp grated ginger

1 tbsp soy sauce

1 tbsp rice wine vinegar

1 tbsp sesame oil

1 tbsp runny honey

4–5 tbsp water or chicken stock

Serves: 4
Prep: 20 minutes

1   Make the dressing: mix together the peanut butter, chilli, garlic and ginger in a bowl. Stir in the soy sauce, vinegar, sesame oil and honey. The mixture will be quite thick. Thin it down with the water or chicken stock, a spoonful at a time, until you reach a pouring consistency.

2   Put all the prepared vegetables and the sprouted seeds in a large bowl. Add the coriander (cilantro) and shredded chicken.

3   Pour the dressing over the salad and toss together gently.

4   Divide the salad between 4 serving plates and scatter with the chilli (if using), sesame seeds and spring onion (scallion) strips. Serve with lime wedges.

Or you can try this...

❖   Add some chopped fresh mint or Thai basil and scatter the salad with a few roasted peanuts.

❖   Instead of a fresh chilli and honey, add 2 tablespoons sweet chilli sauce to the dressing.

Salad dressings

Using seeds and/or their oils in dressings is a marvellous way of adding nutritional value to your daily intake, especially the essential fatty acids and vitamin E that's found in all seeds. Keep the dressings in the refrigerator for up to 2 weeks to maintain their fresh taste and rich benefits.

Satay pumpkin seed dressing

3 tbsp smooth peanut butter
1 tbsp sesame oil
juice of 1 lime
2 tbsp light soy sauce
1 tbsp sweet chilli sauce
1 tsp soft brown sugar
2 tbsp pumpkin seeds
sea salt crystals to taste

Makes: 225ml/8fl oz/scant 1 cup
Prep: 5 minutes

1   Put the peanut butter, sesame oil, lime juice, soy sauce, chilli sauce and sugar in a blender and blitz until smooth.

2   If the dressing is thick, gradually add some water, a spoonful at a time and blitz again. It should be creamy.

3   Stir in the pumpkin seeds and taste. Add a few salt crystals if you wish.

Thai aromatic sesame dressing

grated zest and juice of 1 lime
4 tbsp groundnut (peanut) oil
1 tbsp sesame oil
2 tbsp rice vinegar
2 tbsp nam pla (Thai fish sauce)
1 small red Thai chilli, finely diced
1 garlic clove, finely chopped
1 tsp caster (superfine) sugar
2 tbsp white sesame seeds
1 tbsp chopped mint or Thai basil

Makes: 180ml/6fl oz/¾ cup
Prep: 10 minutes

1 Put all the dressing ingredients in a screw-top jar or any container with a snugly fitting lid. Shake vigorously until well combined and emulsified.

2 You can keep the dressing in the refrigerator for up to a week if you omit the herbs and add them just before serving.

From left: Satay pumpkin seed dressing; Thai aromatic sesame dressing; Tahini dressing; Chilli, lemon and coriander seed dressing; Orange and lemon poppy seed dressing; Toasted sesame honey vinaigrette

Tahini dressing

3 tbsp tahini
1 garlic clove, finely chopped
1 tsp grated fresh root ginger
grated zest and juice of ½ lemon
1 tbsp light soy sauce
½ tsp runny honey
4–5 tbsp warm water
2 tsp sesame oil
a handful of flat-leaf parsley, finely chopped
2 tbsp toasted sesame seeds
salt and freshly ground black pepper

Makes: 150ml/¼ pint/generous ½ cup
Prep: 10 minutes

1   Give the tahini a stir and spoon into a blender with
    the garlic, ginger, lemon zest and juice, soy sauce and
    honey. Blitz until smooth.

2   Add the warm water, a spoonful at a time, and blitz
    until the dressing has a creamy consistency.

3   Transfer to a jug and stir in the sesame oil, parsley
    and sesame seeds. Season to taste.

4   You can keep the dressing in the refrigerator for
    2–3 days in a sealed container.

Chilli, lemon and coriander seed dressing

2 tbsp coriander seeds
1 red chilli, seeded and chopped
2.5cm/1in piece fresh root ginger, peeled and chopped
2 garlic cloves, chopped
grated zest and juice of 2 lemons
6 tbsp fruity green olive oil
a small bunch of coriander (cilantro), finely chopped
salt and freshly ground black pepper

Makes: 225ml/8fl oz/scant 1 cup
Prep: 10 minutes

1   Put the coriander seeds, chilli, ginger and garlic in a pestle
    and mortar and grind to a thick paste.

2   Transfer the paste to a bowl and stir in the lemon zest
    and juice. Gradually add the olive oil, stirring all the time,
    until thickened and smooth.

3   Stir in the coriander (cilantro) and season to taste with a
    little salt and pepper.

NOTE: *If the dressing is too sharp for your taste,
sweeten it with a pinch of sugar or a teaspoon
of runny honey or agave nectar.*

Orange and lemon poppy seed dressing

100ml/3½fl oz/scant ½ cup avocado or grapeseed oil
1 tbsp cider vinegar
juice of 1 large orange
juice of 1 lemon
2 tsp Dijon mustard
1 tbsp agave nectar or runny honey
2 spring onions (scallions), very thinly sliced
1½ tbsp poppy seeds
salt and freshly ground black pepper

Makes: 225ml/8fl oz/scant 1 cup
Prep: 10 minutes

1   Whisk together the oil, vinegar and fruit juice in a bowl.

2   Whisk in the mustard and agave nectar or honey until
    well combined.

3   Stir in the spring onions (scallions) and poppy seeds and
    season to taste with a little salt and pepper.

4   Unless using straight away, transfer the dressing to
    a sealed container or screw-top jar and keep in the
    refrigerator for up to 1 week.

TIP: *You can make the dressing more creamy by
whisking in 1 tablespoon mayonnaise.*

Toasted sesame honey vinaigrette

2 tbsp black and/or white sesame seeds
3 tbsp sunflower oil
1 tbsp toasted sesame oil
2 tbsp rice vinegar
2 tbsp light soy sauce
juice of 1 lime
1 garlic clove, finely chopped
1 tsp grated fresh root ginger
2 tbsp runny honey
a few sprigs of coriander (cilantro), finely chopped

Makes: 150ml/¼ pint/generous ½ cup
Prep: 10 minutes
Cook: 2–3 minutes

1   Place a dry heavy frying pan (skillet) over a medium
    heat and when it's hot, add the sesame seeds. Toast
    for 2–3 minutes, turning and shaking them gently a
    few times, until golden brown. Remove immediately
    and cool. Watch the pan carefully as they can burn if
    left too long.

2   Put the remaining dressing ingredients in a screw-top
    jar or any container with a snugly fitting lid. Add the
    cool sesame seeds and shake vigorously until well
    combined and emulsified.

3   You can keep the dressing in the refrigerator for up
    to a week if you omit the herbs and add them just
    before serving.

Seedy suppers

This healthy dish is equally good eaten warm from the oven or cold the following day. It makes a surprisingly filling supper dish. This recipe is suitable for high-protein diets, since buckwheat is higher in protein than rice. It helps maintain blood-sugar levels owing to its fibre content, making it a great supper dish for diabetics.

Buckwheat-stuffed Mediterranean vegetables

2 medium aubergines (eggplants)

2 red or yellow (bell) peppers

3 tbsp olive oil plus extra for drizzling

150g/5oz/1 cup buckwheat

1 small red onion, diced

2 garlic cloves, crushed

3 tomatoes, diced

a small bunch of flat-leaf parsley, finely chopped

25g/1oz/¼ cup pine nuts

grated zest and juice of 1 lemon

100g/3½oz/scant ½ cup diced feta cheese

salt and freshly ground black pepper

Serves: 4
Prep: 15 minutes
Cook: 30 minutes

1   Preheat the oven to 200°C, 400°F, gas mark 6.

2   Cut the aubergines (eggplants) and (bell) peppers in half through the stalk. Remove the white ribs and seeds from inside the peppers. Place them all, cut-side up, on a baking (cookie) sheet and drizzle generously with olive oil.

3   Bake in the preheated oven for about 20 minutes until tender. Remove from the oven and cool a little, but leave the oven on.

4   Meanwhile, cook the buckwheat according to the instructions on the packet. Heat the remaining olive oil in a frying pan (skillet) and cook the red onion and garlic over a low heat for 10–15 minutes, stirring occasionally, until softened but not coloured. Stir in the diced tomatoes and parsley and cook gently for 4–5 minutes.

5   Toast the pine nuts in a dry frying pan (skillet) over a low heat for 2–3 minutes, stirring a few times, until golden brown and toasted. Remove from the heat immediately.

6   Scoop the cooked flesh out of the aubergines (eggplants) and dice it. Add to the onion and tomato mixture with the cooked buckwheat, pine nuts, lemon zest and juice and feta, and stir well. Season to taste with salt and pepper.

7   Pile the mixture into the baked aubergine (eggplant) and (bell) pepper shells and return to the oven for 8–10 minutes. Serve warm or cold with salad.

Or you can try this...

❖   Turn up the heat by adding a diced chilli or a dash of harissa or hot pepper sauce to the buckwheat filling mixture.

❖   Instead of using feta, sprinkle the stuffed vegetables with grated Parmesan or Cheddar cheese before putting them back into the hot oven for the final 10 minutes.

Dhal is so simple to make – filling, spicy and satisfying, it is comfort food at its best. The cumin and coriander seeds provide abundant anti-inflammatory antioxidants whilst the mustard seeds in the chutney are rich in magnesium, which may help to reduce menopausal symptoms.

Dhal with seedy coconut chutney

2 tbsp coconut oil

1 red onion, finely chopped

4 garlic cloves, crushed

1 tsp cumin seeds

1 tsp crushed coriander seeds

1 tsp ground turmeric

1 tsp ground cinnamon

1 green chilli, finely chopped

1 tsp finely grated fresh root ginger

200g/7oz/1 cup red split lentils (dry weight), washed and drained

1 x 400ml/14fl oz can reduced-fat coconut milk

300ml/½ pint/1¼ cups vegetable stock

a handful of coriander (cilantro), chopped

juice of 1 lime

salt and freshly ground black pepper

boiled rice, naan or chapatis to serve

Seedy coconut chutney:

50g/2oz/¾ cup freshly grated coconut or desiccated coconut

100ml/3½fl oz/scant ½ cup boiling water

1 tsp coconut oil

1 tsp black mustard seeds

1 tsp cumin seeds

4 curry leaves

1 red chilli, diced

Serves: 4
Prep: 10 minutes
Cook: 30 minutes

1 Heat the coconut oil in a heavy pan and set over a low heat. Add the onion and garlic and cook gently, stirring occasionally, for 6–8 minutes until tender.

2 Add the cumin and coriander seeds, ground spices, chilli and ginger. Stir well and cook gently for 2–3 minutes.

3 Add the lentils and stir well. Pour in the coconut milk and stock and bring to the boil. Reduce the heat, cover the pan and simmer gently for about 20–25 minutes, until the lentils are cooked and tender. Check the pan occasionally and add more stock if the lentils are starting to stick to the bottom of the pan.

4 Remove from the heat and stir in the chopped coriander (cilantro) and lime juice. Season to taste with salt and pepper.

5 While the dhal is cooking, make the seedy coconut chutney: put the coconut in a bowl and pour over the boiling water. Set aside to soak for at least 15 minutes, then drain well. Heat the coconut oil in a pan and add the mustard and cumin seeds, curry leaves and chilli. As soon as they splutter and crackle after about 1 minute, tip them over the coconut and mix well.

6 Serve the dhal topped with the coconut chutney and with some boiled rice, naan or chapatis.

Or you can try this...

❖ Just before serving, mix in some baby spinach leaves. They will wilt and turn bright green in the hot dhal.

❖ Add chopped mint or coriander (cilantro) to the chutney, a dash of lime juice or 1 teaspoon tamarind paste.

Seared on the outside to give a crunchy crust, and succulent but firm-textured on the inside, this recipe has everything you could wish for in a burger – plus colour and seedy goodness in abundance. The seeds provide additional fibre and sustain blood-sugar levels to contribute to restorative sleep.

Seedy root vegetable burgers

300g/11oz sweet potatoes, peeled and diced

1 medium swede (rutabaga), peeled and diced

175g/6oz kale, shredded

3 tbsp olive oil

6 spring onions (scallions), finely chopped

2 garlic cloves, finely chopped

a small bunch of chives, snipped

60g/2oz roasted nuts, e.g. hazelnuts, macadamias or almonds, chopped

2 tbsp plain (all-purpose) flour

2 tsp wholegrain mustard

75g/3oz mixed seeds, e.g. pumpkin, sunflower, black and white sesame

8 multi-seed rolls

sliced tomato, rocket (arugula) and mayonnaise to serve

salt and freshly ground black pepper

Serves: 8
Prep: 20 minutes
Chill: 20 minutes
Cook: 30 minutes

1 Cook the sweet potatoes and swede in a large pan of boiling salted water for about 15 minutes until tender. Drain well.

2 Meanwhile, cook the kale in a pan of boiling water for 4–5 minutes and drain well.

3 Coarsely chop the kale. Using a potato masher, roughly crush the sweet potatoes and swede – the mash shouldn't be too smooth.

4 Heat 1 tablespoon olive oil in a small frying pan (skillet) over a medium heat and cook the spring onions (scallions) and garlic until softened but not coloured. Stir in the chives.

5 Transfer to a bowl and mix in the crushed root vegetables, kale and nuts. Stir in the flour and mustard, and season to taste.

6 Divide into 8 portions and shape each one into a burger with your hands. Coat them with the mixed seeds, pressing down to cover them evenly all over. Chill in the refrigerator for at least 20 minutes.

7 When you're ready to cook the burgers, heat the remaining oil in a frying pan (skillet) over a low to medium heat and cook them for 3–4 minutes or until the undersides are golden brown. Flip them over and cook the other side. Remove from the pan and drain on kitchen paper (towel).

8 Split the rolls and lightly toast them. Serve the burgers in the rolls with tomato, rocket (arugula) and a dollop of mayonnaise.

Or you can try this...

❖ Vary the root vegetables and use diced potatoes, parsnips or celeriac.

Try not to eat this chutney straight away. If you can bear to put it away in a cupboard for two or three weeks before opening, it will taste even better. It's great with hard cheeses or some boiled ham. The plethora of antioxidant-rich seeds complements the lycopene (another antioxidant) in the cooked tomatoes, making this an excellent relish for supporting immunity.

Seedy Indian tomato chutney

1 tsp fenugreek seeds

6 tbsp sunflower oil

1 tbsp cumin seeds

2 tbsp black mustard seeds

2.5cm/1in piece fresh root ginger, peeled and diced

3 garlic cloves, crushed

1 red chilli, diced

1.5kg/3lb tomatoes, skinned and chopped

450g/1lb/2 cups granulated sugar

300ml/½ pint/1¼ cups malt vinegar

1 tsp salt

Makes: about 1kg/2lb 2oz
Prep: 15 minutes
Cook: 1–1¼ hours

1 Toast the fenugreek seeds in a dry frying pan (skillet) over a medium heat for 1–2 minutes, stirring occasionally. Remove from the pan and set aside to cool for a few minutes.

2 Heat the oil in a large heavy-based saucepan and cook the cumin, mustard and fenugreek seeds over a low heat for 2–3 minutes. Stir in the ginger, garlic and chilli and cook for 2–3 minutes. You should have a pungent, spicy, aromatic mixture.

3 Add the tomatoes and sugar and simmer gently for 15 minutes, stirring occasionally to dissolve the sugar. Stir in the vinegar and salt and simmer gently until the mixture thickens to a syrupy chutney-like consistency without any liquid. Be patient – this might take anything from 40 minutes up to an hour. Stir the chutney regularly to prevent it from catching and burning on the bottom of the pan.

4 While the chutney is cooking, sterilize some jars by popping some clean ones (lids off) into a very low oven at 110°C, 225°F, gas mark ¼ for about 20 minutes, then turn the oven off and leave the jars in the oven until you're ready to fill them.

5 Ladle the hot chutney into the hot sterilized jars and half-screw on the lids. When they are cool, tighten the lids and store in a cool dark place.

Or you can try this...

❖ Cook a diced onion or two with the seeds and spices before adding the tomatoes.

❖ Add some chunks of golden pumpkin or plump sultanas (golden raisins).

Even the most committed meat eater will enjoy this delicious vegetarian gratin. You can prepare it an hour in advance (up to stage 5 below) and then put it in the oven 15 minutes before serving supper. Pumpkin seeds contain potent essential fats – omega-3 and -6 – as well as anti-microbial properties that help to protect the digestive tract.

Butternut squash and goat's cheese bake with pumpkin seeds

900g/2lb butternut squash, peeled, seeded and cut into chunks

leaves stripped from a few sprigs of thyme

2 tsp cumin seeds

black pepper

250ml/8fl oz/1 cup vegetable stock

100ml/3½fl oz/scant ½ cup half-fat crème fraîche

80g/3oz soft goat's cheese, e.g. chèvre

2 tbsp pumpkin seeds

4 tbsp fresh breadcrumbs

Tomato sauce:

2 tbsp olive oil

1 large onion, finely chopped

2 garlic cloves, crushed

1 x 400g/14oz can chopped tomatoes

1 tbsp tomato paste

drizzle of balsamic vinegar

salt and freshly ground black pepper

Serves: 4
Prep: 10 minutes
Cook: 45 minutes

1 Preheat the oven to 180°C, 350°F, gas mark 4.

2 Arrange the squash in a large ovenproof dish and scatter over the thyme leaves and cumin seeds. Season with a little black pepper and pour the stock over the top. Bake in the preheated oven for about 30 minutes until just tender but not soft.

3 Meanwhile, make the tomato sauce. Heat the oil in a large frying pan (skillet) and cook the onion and garlic over a low heat, stirring occasionally, for about 10 minutes until the onions are softened but not coloured.

4 Stir in the tomatoes and tomato paste and simmer gently for 10 minutes or so until the sauce reduces and becomes thick and pulpy. Add a good dash of balsamic vinegar to sweeten it, and season to taste with salt and pepper.

5 Remove the cooked squash from the oven and spoon the tomato sauce over and around it. Dot the top with spoonfuls of crème fraîche and goat's cheese, then sprinkle with pumpkin seeds and breadcrumbs.

6 Turn up the oven to 200°C, 400°F, gas mark 6 and cook for 15 minutes until the breadcrumbs are crisp and golden and the sauce is bubbling up.

7 Serve hot or lukewarm with a crisp salad.

Or you can try this...

❖ Use swede, pumpkin, parsnips, sweet potato or even beetroot (beets) instead of squash.

❖ Spoonfuls of mascarpone would make a good creamy alternative to goat's cheese.

The trick to making a really flavoursome onion tart is to cook the onions as slowly as possible over a very low heat until they have a melting consistency, a sweet flavour, and become a deep golden brown. Caraway seeds contain potent immune-supporting minerals zinc and manganese as well as vitamins A, C and E, which all help to reduce indigestion.

Caramelized onion tart with caraway seed crust

Caraway seed pastry (pie-crust):

1 tbsp caraway seeds

300g/11oz/3 generous cups plain (all-purpose) flour

a pinch of salt

a pinch of cayenne

150g/5oz/generous ½ cup butter, diced

1 free-range egg yolk, beaten

cold water to mix

Filling:

25g/1oz/2 tbsp butter plus extra for greasing

2 tbsp olive oil

4 onions, thinly sliced

1 tbsp caraway seeds

300ml/½ pint/1¼ cups single (light) cream or milk

3 free-range eggs, beaten

a pinch of freshly grated nutmeg

100g/3½oz/1 cup grated cheese, e.g. Emmental or Gruyère

a small bunch of chives, snipped

salt and freshly ground black pepper

Serves: 6
Prep: 25 minutes
Chill: 30 minutes
Cook: 1¼ hours

1 Preheat the oven to 190°C, 375°F, gas mark 5. Lightly butter a deep 23cm/9in loose-bottomed tart tin (spring-form tart pan).

2 Toast the caraway seeds in a dry frying pan (skillet) set over a low heat for 1–2 minutes, stirring occasionally. Remove and cool for a few minutes, then grind coarsely in a spice grinder or pestle and mortar.

3 Make the pastry (pie-crust): sift the flour, salt and cayenne into a large bowl. Stir in the ground caraway seeds. Add the diced butter and rub it in with your fingertips until the mixture resembles breadcrumbs. Stir in the beaten egg yolk and then enough cold water to bind everything together and make a ball of dough that leaves the sides of the bowl clean.

4 Wrap the dough in some cling film (plastic wrap) or place in a polythene bag and leave to rest in the refrigerator for at least 30 minutes.

5 Meanwhile, heat the butter and olive oil in a large heavy frying pan (skillet) over a low heat and cook the onions, stirring occasionally, for about 20 minutes or until they are really soft, tender and turning golden brown. Stir in the caraway seeds.

6 Roll out the pastry (pie-crust) to a large circle on a lightly floured surface and use to line the prepared tart tin, leaving any excess hanging over the edges. Line the tart with some baking parchment and fill with baking beans. Place on a baking (cookie) sheet and bake 'blind' in the preheated oven for 15 minutes. Remove the paper and beans and pop back in the oven for 5–10 minutes until cooked. Set aside for 5 minutes before neatening the top edge of the pastry (pie-crust) case.

7 Fill with the onion mixture. Beat the cream or milk with the eggs, nutmeg and a little seasoning. Stir in the grated cheese and chives and pour over the onions.

8 Bake in the oven for about 25–30 minutes until the filling is just set and golden brown. Serve warm or cold cut into slices.

Or you can try this...

❖ Instead of making the pastry (pie-crust) with caraway seeds, add 2 teaspoons toasted fennel seeds and a pinch of English mustard powder, or 2 tablespoons poppy seeds.

This quick and fresh green supper dish is ideal for spring and early summer when the new tender asparagus comes into season. The iron levels in poppy seeds, together with their abundant B-complex vitamins, contribute to the overall energy-producing content of this dish.

Asparagus and poppy seed pasta ribbons

50g/2oz/½ cup pine nuts

450g/1lb tagliatelle, fettuccine or pappardelle

300g/11oz asparagus

250ml/9fl oz/1 cup crème fraîche

grated zest and juice of 1 small lemon

50g/2oz baby spinach leaves

2 tbsp poppy seeds

30g/1oz/ ¼ cup shaved or grated Parmesan cheese

salt and freshly ground black pepper

Serves: 4
Prep: 10 minutes
Cook: 10 minutes

1 Toast the pine nuts in a dry frying pan (skillet) set over a low to medium heat, stirring occasionally, for 1–2 minutes until uniformly golden brown. Remove from the pan and cool.

2 Cook the pasta in a large pan of salted boiling water according to the instructions on the packet.

3 Trim the woody ends off the asparagus and cut the stems into 2.5cm/1in pieces. Cook them in a steamer basket placed over a pan of boiling water for about 4 minutes, until they are just tender but still retain some crispness.

4 Drain the pasta, reserving 2 tablespoons of the cooking water. Put it back in the warm pan and stir in the crème fraîche and lemon zest.

5 Add the toasted pine nuts, spinach, asparagus and poppy seeds, together with the reserved cooking liquid and the lemon juice. Lightly toss everything together and season to taste.

6 Divide the pasta between 4 shallow serving bowls and sprinkle with the Parmesan.

Or you can try this...

❖ For a lower-calorie version, use half-fat crème fraîche or even stir in some 0% fat Greek yoghurt.

❖ For a more distinctive flavour, use fennel seeds and some chopped feathery fennel fronds.

Salmon, an excellent source of vitamins B6 and B12 (and much else) is great combined with Japanese flavours in a quick stir-fry. The zinc and selenium in sesame seeds help make this a wonderfully immune-supporting, hormone-balancing supper dish.

Stir-fried salmon and sesame noodles

50ml/2fl oz/¼ cup mirin

2 tbsp soy sauce

500g/1lb 2oz skinned salmon fillets, cut into strips or chunks

300g/11oz egg noodles (dry weight)

2 tsp sesame oil

2.5cm/1in piece fresh root ginger, peeled and grated

1 yellow (bell) pepper, seeded and cut into strips

2 carrots, cut into matchsticks

a bunch of spring onions (scallions), sliced diagonally

200g/7oz pak choi (bok choy), roughly chopped

100g/3½oz/1 cup bean sprouts

grated zest and juice of 1 lime

1 tbsp black or white sesame seeds

Serves: 4
Prep: 10 minutes
Marinate: 10–15 minutes
Cook: 8 minutes

1 Mix the mirin and soy sauce together in a shallow bowl. Add the salmon and stir to coat. Set aside for 10–15 minutes to marinate.

2 Cook the noodles according to the instructions on the packet, and drain.

3 Meanwhile heat the sesame oil in a wok or deep frying pan (skillet) over a medium to high heat. Add the salmon and toss gently for 2–3 minutes until browned all over.

4 Add the ginger, yellow (bell) pepper, carrots, spring onions (scallions), pak choi (bok choy) and bean sprouts and stir-fry for about 3 minutes. The vegetables should still be slightly crunchy.

5 Add the cooked egg noodles, lime juice and zest and sesame seeds and stir-fry for 1 minute.

6 Divide between 4 shallow serving bowls and serve immediately.

Or you can try this...

❖ Add some heat with a diced or shredded chilli or a spoonful of sweet chilli sauce.

❖ Substitute teriyaki sauce for the soy sauce.

Try this quick and simple curry for a speedy supper when you don't have much time to cook. Both the coriander and mustard seeds provide a good supply of B vitamins for muscular and brain energy, whilst pomegranate seeds have extremely high stores of vitamin C for supporting immunity.

Prawn and tomato curry

1 large aubergine (eggplant)

5 tbsp sunflower oil

2 onions, diced

3 garlic cloves, crushed

1 green chilli, diced

5cm/2in piece fresh root ginger, peeled and chopped

1 tsp ground turmeric

1 tsp ground coriander (cilantro)

2 tsp crushed coriander seeds

1 tbsp black mustard seeds

350g/12oz tomatoes, chopped

1 x 400ml/14fl oz can reduced-fat coconut milk

450g/1lb raw shelled tiger prawns (shrimp)

a small bunch of coriander (cilantro), chopped

seeds of 1 small pomegranate

salt and freshly ground black pepper

boiled rice and seedy Indian tomato chutney (*see page 131*) to serve

Serves: 4
Prep: 15 minutes
Cook: 30 minutes

1. Cut the aubergine (eggplant) into slices and then cut each slice in half or into quarters. Drizzle with 2 tablespoons oil.

2. Heat a griddle pan, add the aubergine (eggplant), a few pieces at a time, and cook over a medium heat until golden brown on both sides. Remove and drain on kitchen paper (towel).

3. Meanwhile, heat the remaining oil in a large saucepan or deep frying pan (skillet) and cook the onions, garlic and chilli over a low to medium heat for about 8–10 minutes until softened.

4. Add the ginger, ground spices and coriander and mustard seeds, and cook for 2 minutes, stirring, to release their aroma.

5. Stir in the tomatoes and coconut milk and simmer gently for 15 minutes until reduced and thickened.

6. Add the aubergine (eggplant) and prawns (shrimp) and cook for a further 2–3 minutes until the prawns (shrimp) are pink on both sides. Stir in most of the coriander (cilantro) and season to taste.

7. Serve the curry with some boiled rice, sprinkled with pomegranate seeds and the remaining coriander (cilantro), with the seedy Indian tomato chutney.

Or you can try this...

❖ Vegetarians can omit the prawns (shrimp) and add some green beans or courgettes (zucchini) or even some cubed tofu or paneer.

❖ Make the curry spicier by adding a teaspoon of ground cinnamon, garam masala or curry paste.

This is an easy and relatively quick dish to make – don't be deterred by the long list of ingredients. It's totally delicious and healthy, too, with a veritable jackpot of seeds. Mustard, cumin, fennel and fenugreek all contribute their essential fatty acid content (DHA) to the omega-3 fatty acid (EPA) found in fish, combining to provide a great all-round anti-inflammatory feast.

Roasted fish fillets with a seedy Indian crust

1 tbsp coriander seeds

2 tsp black mustard seeds

1 tsp yellow mustard seeds

1 tbsp fennel seeds

½ tsp fenugreek seeds

1 tsp ground turmeric

a pinch of ground ginger

a good pinch of sea salt crystals

4 x 175g/6oz skinned white fish fillets

sunflower oil for brushing

seedy Indian tomato chutney
(see page 131) or raita to serve

Saag aloo:

2 tbsp sunflower oil

1 onion, chopped

2.5cm/1in piece fresh root ginger,
peeled and diced

2 garlic cloves, crushed

1 red chilli, seeded and shredded

1 tsp black mustard seeds

1 tsp cumin seeds

½ tsp fennel seeds

½ tsp ground turmeric

400g/14oz potatoes, peeled and cut
into cubes

300g/10oz baby spinach leaves

Serves: 4
Prep: 15 minutes
Cook: 20 minutes

1 Preheat the oven to 180°C, 350°F, gas mark 4.

2 Place a dry frying pan (skillet) over a medium heat. When it's hot, add the coriander and mustard seeds and cook for 1 minute or until the mustard seeds begin to pop. Stir in the fennel and fenugreek seeds and heat through for about 30 seconds until they release their aroma. Remove the seeds and set aside to cool.

3 Grind the toasted seeds coarsely in a pestle and mortar and stir in the ground spices and sea salt crystals. Grind again.

4 Sprinkle the spicy seed mixture over the fish fillets and press lightly into them. Place the coated fish on a lightly oiled baking (cookie) sheet. Bake for about 15–20 minutes until the fish is thoroughly cooked and the crust is crisp. Check them after 10 minutes and turn them over.

5 While the fish is cooking, make the saag aloo. Heat the oil in a large frying pan (skillet) over a medium heat and cook the onion, ginger and garlic for 4–5 minutes. Add the chilli, seeds, turmeric and potatoes and cook for 5 minutes, stirring occasionally.

6 Add 2–3 tablespoons water, then cover the pan, reduce the heat and cook for 8–10 minutes until the potatoes are tender. Stir in the spinach and let it wilt. As soon as it turns bright green, it's ready.

7 Serve the fish fillets and saag aloo with a spoonful of chutney or raita.

Or you can try this...

❖ Make the seedy crust hotter by adding some ground cayenne, chilli powder or dried chilli flakes to the mixture.

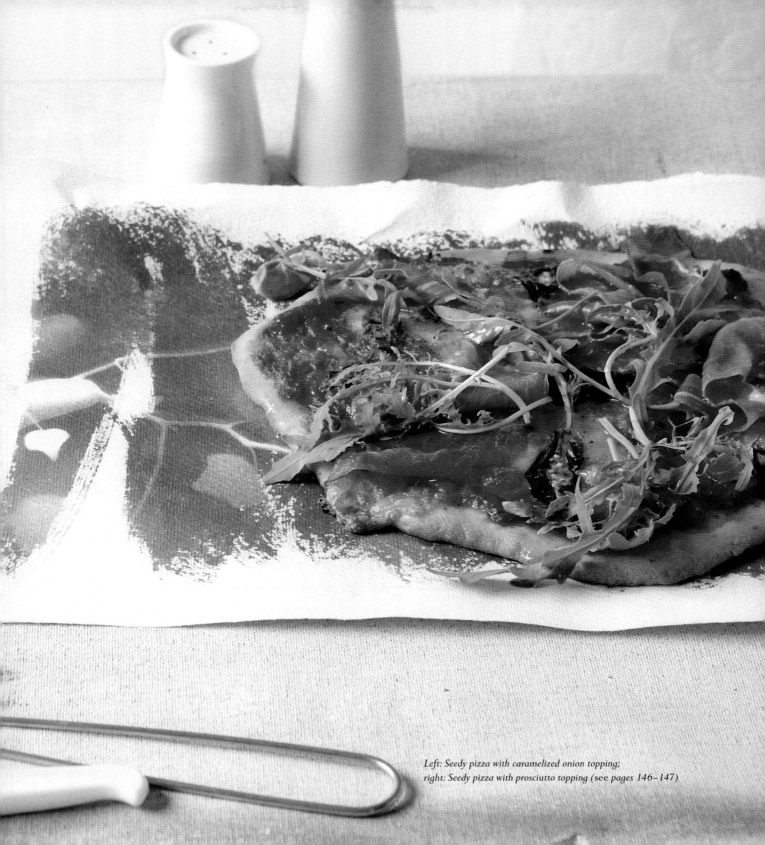

Left: Seedy pizza with caramelized onion topping;
right: Seedy pizza with prosciutto topping (see pages 146–147)

This recipe makes enough dough and tomato sauce for 4 pizzas. Although it's time-consuming to make the base, the superior taste makes it well worth the effort. You can make double the quantity of dough and store it in the refrigerator in a polythene bag for several days. The seeds in the dough add fibre and protein, making the dish especially suitable for diabetics and people following a higher-protein diet.

Seedy pizza with prosciutto topping

Tomato sauce:

3 tbsp olive oil

1 onion, finely chopped

1 x 400g/14oz can chopped tomatoes

2–3 tbsp tomato paste

salt and freshly ground black pepper

Pizza dough:

500g/1lb 2oz/5 cups 00 or strong white flour

1 x 7g sachet /scant ½ oz fast-action yeast

1 tsp sea salt

300ml/½ pint/1¼ cups warm water

2 tbsp fennel, hemp, chia or sesame seeds

leaves stripped from a few sprigs of thyme or rosemary

Topping:

350g/12oz mozzarella, torn into pieces or cut into cubes

a few basil leaves

olive oil for drizzling

80g/3oz thinly sliced Parma ham, torn into strips

2 large handfuls of wild rocket (arugula)

Serves: 4–6
Prep: 30 minutes
Rising: 1–2 hours
Cook: 30–35 minutes

1   Make the tomato sauce. You can do this the day before and keep it in an airtight jar or container in the refrigerator until you're ready to make and assemble the pizzas. Heat the olive oil in a large frying pan (skillet) over a low heat and cook the onion, stirring occasionally, for about 10 minutes until softened and translucent, not coloured. Add the tomatoes and tomato paste and let the sauce simmer for 10 minutes or so until it reduces and thickens. Season with salt and pepper and set aside to cool.

2   Make the pizza dough: put the flour in a large mixing bowl with the yeast and salt. Make a well in the centre and pour in most of the warm water. Mix to a soft dough, drawing in the flour from the sides with your hand. Alternatively, use a food mixer fitted with a dough hook. If the dough is too dry, add a little more warm water.

3   Put the ball of dough on a well-floured work surface and knead by hand for 10 minutes. Alternatively, do it in a food processor fitted with a dough hook in half the time. It should feel smooth, silky and elastic.

4   Put the dough in a large lightly oiled bowl and cover with cling film (plastic wrap) or a damp cloth. Leave in a warm place for 1–2 hours until it doubles in size.

5   Preheat the oven to 230°C, 450°F, gas mark 8. Knock down the dough: put it on a lightly floured surface and fold it repeatedly in on itself using the heels of your hands until it is smooth and all the air is 'knocked' out of it. Knead it lightly, adding the seeds and herbs as you do so. Keep kneading until they are mixed in and distributed throughout the dough. Cut it into 4 equal-sized pieces and either roll each one out thinly into a large disc, or stretch the dough out between your raised hands to the desired thinness. Place the pizza bases on baking (cookie) sheets.

6   Spread the tomato sauce thinly over the pizza bases leaving a 2.5cm/1in border around the edge for the crust to rise. Scatter the mozzarella over the top. Add the basil and a drizzle of olive oil.

7   Cook in the preheated oven for about 12–15 minutes until the pizza bases are crisp and the cheese has melted. Topped with the Parma ham and rocket (arugula).

These pizzas have a Sicilian 'agrodolce' (sweet and sour) flavour due to the natural sweetness of the onions and sultanas (golden raisins) being offset by the vinegar. The fennel seeds add a delicious faintly aniseed flavour to the topping.

Seedy pizza with caramelized onion topping

1 quantity tomato sauce (see opposite)

1 quantity seedy pizza dough (see opposite)

Topping:

3 tbsp olive oil plus extra for drizzling

4 onions, thinly sliced

2 tbsp fennel seeds

4 tbsp pine nuts

80g/3oz/½ cup sultanas (golden raisins)

a few drops of balsamic vinegar

350g/12oz mozzarella, torn into pieces or cubed

salt and freshly ground black pepper

Serves: 4–6
Prep: 30 minutes
Rise: 1–2 hours
Cook: 1 hour

1   Heat the olive oil in a large frying pan (skillet) over a low heat. Add the onions and cook very gently and slowly, turning occasionally, for about 20 minutes until they are really tender and starting to turn golden and caramelize. Stir in the fennel seeds and cook for 1–2 minutes.

2   Remove from the heat and stir in the pine nuts and sultanas (golden raisins). Season to taste with salt and pepper and add a few drops of balsamic vinegar.

3   Roll out the pizza dough to make 4 bases (*see* stage 5 opposite) and place them on baking (cookie) sheets. Spread the tomato sauce thinly over them, leaving a 2.5cm/1in border around the edge for the crust to rise.

4   Divide the onion mixture between the pizzas and spread over the sauce; scatter the mozzarella over the top. Add a drizzle of olive oil.

5   Cook in a preheated oven at 230°C, 450°F, gas mark 8 for about 12–15 minutes until the pizza bases are crisp and the cheese has melted. Serve immediately.

Or you can try this...

❖   Break an egg into the centre of each pizza before cooking.

❖   Mix some baby spinach leaves into the onion mixture.

Aromatic sesame seeds make a flavoursome crunchy coating for chicken. The additional zinc and selenium in the sesame seeds make this dish an immune-boosting powerhouse.

Sesame seed-coated chicken breasts

2 tbsp soy sauce

1 tbsp hoisin sauce

1 tbsp runny honey

2 tbsp sunflower oil

a pinch of salt

4 chicken breasts, skinned and cut into thick slices

100g/3½oz/scant ¾ cup white sesame seeds

2.5cm/1in piece fresh root ginger, peeled and shredded

2 garlic cloves, thinly sliced

2 red chillies, seeded and shredded

1 tsp cumin seeds

a bunch of spring onions (scallions), diagonally sliced

450g/1lb baby spinach leaves

steamed rice or cooked rice noodles to serve

Serves: 4
Prep: 10 minutes
Cook: 10 minutes

1 In a large bowl, mix together the soy and hoisin sauces, honey, and 1 teaspoon of oil. Stir in the salt, then add the chicken slices. Turn them until they are coated all over with the mixture.

2 Put the sesame seeds in a shallow dish. Dip the chicken slices into the seeds until they are thoroughly coated.

3 Heat most of the remaining oil in a wok or deep frying pan (skillet) over a medium heat. When it's hot, add the sesame-coated chicken and cook for about 3 minutes each side until the coating is richly browned and slightly sticky, and the chicken is cooked through.

4 Meanwhile, in another pan heat the remaining oil and stir-fry the ginger, garlic, chillies and cumin seeds over a medium to high heat for 2 minutes or until they start to crackle. Add the spring onions (scallions) and spinach and stir-fry briskly until the spinach wilts.

5 Serve immediately with the sesame-coated chicken and some rice or noodles.

Or you can try this...

❖ Use chicken thighs or wings instead of sliced breasts – but they will take longer to cook. Cook them in a preheated oven at 220°C, 425°F, gas mark 7 for 25–30 minutes.

❖ Try adding a squeeze of lime or lemon juice to the spinach or a dash of soy sauce or nam pla (Thai fish sauce).

This warm salad is a real treat if you love rare steak. The pomegranate seeds offer a veritable feast of antioxidants as well as vitamin K, which is essential for the body's natural blood-clotting mechanism.

Steak and squash salad with pomegranate seeds

2 tbsp coriander seeds

2 tbsp cumin seeds

1 tsp nigella seeds

1 large butternut squash, seeded and cut into strips

8 tbsp olive oil

675g/1½lb piece of very lean steak, e.g. fillet, sirloin or onglet (hanger), fat removed

25g/1oz wild rocket (arugula)

seeds of 1 small pomegranate

sea salt crystals and freshly ground black pepper

Dressing:

2 tbsp red wine vinegar

3 tbsp pomegranate molasses

1 tbsp Dijon mustard

2 tsp runny honey

100ml/3½fl oz/scant ½ cup olive oil

salt and freshly ground black pepper

Serves: 4
Prep: 15 minutes
Cook: 40 minutes
Rest: 10 minutes

NOTE: *If using onglet (hanger) steak, it may take longer to cook – choose a piece that isn't too thick.*

1 Preheat the oven to 200°C, 400°F, gas mark 6.

2 In a pestle and mortar, coarsely grind the coriander, cumin and nigella seeds.

3 Place the squash in a roasting pan and sprinkle the seeds over the top. Drizzle with 4 tablespoons olive oil and season with salt and pepper.

4 Roast in the preheated oven for 25–35 minutes, turning the squash once or twice, until tender and golden brown outside. Remove and set aside to cool.

5 Make the dressing: whisk the vinegar, pomegranate molasses, mustard and honey together. Gradually whisk in the oil and season lightly with salt and pepper.

6 Brush the steak with the remaining oil, rubbing it into both sides, and grind some sea salt and black pepper over the top.

7 Heat a heavy ridged griddle pan over a high heat. When it's really hot, add the steak and sear for 2–3 minutes each side for rare meat. If you like your steak medium-rare to medium, cook it for 4–5 minutes each side. Remove from the pan and set aside for at least 10 minutes.

8 Put the cool squash, rocket (arugula) and most of the pomegranate seeds in a bowl and toss lightly with half of the dressing.

9 Slice the warm steak with a very sharp knife and add to the salad. Pour the remaining dressing over the top and scatter with the reserved pomegranate seeds.

Or you can try this...

❖ Sear lamb fillets in the same way and serve sliced with the dressing.

❖ Add some heat to the salad by whisking a pinch of dried chilli flakes into the dressing.

This typically rustic Italian dish has the slightly aniseed flavour of fennel. The seeds have a mildly diuretic effect, helping to balance the acid-forming effects of the sausage meat and thereby supporting the kidneys.

Fettuccine with spicy sausage and fennel seeds

3 tbsp olive oil

1 large onion, chopped

1 small fennel bulb, trimmed and diced

2 garlic cloves, crushed

2 tsp fennel seeds

400g/14oz Italian spicy sausages

1 x 400g/14oz can chopped tomatoes

1 sprig fresh rosemary

1 tbsp tomato paste

200ml/7fl oz/generous ¾ cup red wine

a handful of flat-leaf parsley, chopped, plus extra to garnish

a few drops of balsamic vinegar

500g/1lb 2oz fettuccine

Parmesan cheese for grating

salt and freshly ground black pepper

Serves: 4
Prep: 10 minutes
Cook: 40 minutes

1 Heat the olive oil in a large saucepan and cook the onion, fennel, garlic and fennel seeds over a low heat, stirring occasionally, for about 10 minutes until softened.

2 Slit open the sausages with a sharp knife and squeeze out the meaty filling. Add to the pan and turn up the heat to medium. Cook for 10 minutes, stirring occasionally and breaking up the sausage meat, until it is golden brown and crisp.

3 Add the tomatoes, rosemary, tomato paste and red wine. Simmer for 15–20 minutes until reduced. Remove the rosemary sprig. Stir in most of the parsley and a few drops of balsamic vinegar. Season to taste with salt and pepper.

4 Meanwhile, cook the fettuccine in a large pan of boiling salted water according to the instructions on the packet. Drain well.

5 Gently toss the fettuccine in the spicy sausage sauce, and divide between 4 shallow serving dishes. Sprinkle with the remaining parsley and serve with grated Parmesan.

Or you can try this...

❖ For a subtler flavour, use white wine instead of red.

❖ If you love fennel, leave out the parsley and use finely chopped feathery fronds of fennel herb instead.

This quick chilli is made with canned beans and tomatoes from the store cupboard. You can make it a day in advance and keep it covered overnight in the refrigerator to reheat for supper the following day. It also freezes well. The cumin seeds add an anti-inflammatory quotient, so the chilli won't irritate even the most sensitive stomach.

Quinoa and minced beef chilli with cumin seeds

1 tbsp sunflower oil

2 onions, chopped

2 garlic cloves, crushed

1 red chilli, finely chopped

500g/1lb 2oz/2¼ cups minced (ground) low-fat beef

1 tbsp cumin seeds

1 tsp ground cinnamon

1 tsp chipotle paste or chilli powder

2 x 400g/14oz cans chopped tomatoes

300ml/½ pint/1¼ cups beef stock

1 x 400g/14oz can black beans or red kidney beans

175g/6oz/1 cup quinoa

a handful of coriander (cilantro), roughly chopped

1 ripe avocado, peeled, stoned (pitted) and cubed

grated zest and juice of 1 lime

4 tbsp sour cream

1 tbsp pumpkin seeds

salt and freshly ground black pepper

Serves: 4
Prep: 10 minutes
Cook: 45–50 minutes

1 Heat the oil in a large saucepan and cook the onions, garlic and chilli, stirring occasionally, over a low to medium heat for 6–8 minutes until softened.

2 Add the minced beef, cumin seeds, cinnamon and chipotle paste or chilli powder. Cook for about 5 minutes, stirring occasionally, until the beef is browned all over.

3 Add the tomatoes and beef stock and simmer gently for 25–30 minutes until the sauce reduces and thickens. Stir in the canned beans and cook gently for 5 minutes to warm them through. Season with salt and pepper to taste.

4 While the chilli is cooking, cook the quinoa according to the instructions on the packet.

5 Serve the chilli on a bed of quinoa and scatter with the chopped coriander (cilantro) and avocado, tossed in the lime juice and zest. Add a spoonful of sour cream to each serving and sprinkle with pumpkin seeds.

Or you can try this...

❖ Use half-fat crème fraîche instead of sour cream for a lower-fat version.

❖ This also tastes great with boiled or steamed rice or tortillas heated on a hot griddle.

Baking & desserts

These tangy cookies are a great accompaniment to cheese. Top them with hummus or cut them into sticks instead of rounds and use them as dippers. Caraway seeds contain calcium and magnesium, which help to move food through the digestive tract, allowing for the absorption of nutrients. Nigella is a rich source of the omega-rich essential fatty acid known as CLA (conjugated linoleic acid), which helps break down other fats that contribute to weight gain.

Cheesy caraway cookies

250g/9oz/2½ cups plain (all-purpose) flour plus extra for dusting

½ tsp cayenne pepper plus extra for sprinkling

a large pinch of salt

125g/4oz/½ cup chilled butter plus extra for greasing

125g/4oz/generous 1 cup grated Parmesan cheese

3 tbsp caraway seeds

1 tsp nigella seeds

1 large organic egg

cold water to mix

Makes: about 30–40 cookies
Prep: 15 minutes
Chill: 15 minutes
Cook: 10 minutes

1 Preheat the oven to 200°C, 400°F, gas mark 6. Lightly butter 2 baking (cookie) sheets.

2 Sift the flour into a large mixing bowl. Add the cayenne and salt and mix well. Cut the butter into dice and rub into the flour with your fingertips until the mixture resembles fine breadcrumbs. Stir in the Parmesan and seeds.

3 Beat the egg and stir into the mixture. Add some cold water, 1 tablespoon at a time, until everything binds together into a dough that leaves the sides of the bowl clean.

4 Turn the dough out onto a lightly floured board and knead lightly before rolling out thinly about 3mm/¼ in thick. Cut into small rounds with a cookie cutter and arrange on the baking (cookie) sheets. Roll out any leftover dough and cut into more rounds.

5 Cover the sheets with kitchen foil and chill in the refrigerator for at least 15 minutes before dusting lightly with cayenne. Bake in the preheated oven for about 10 minutes until crisp and golden.

6 Cool the cookies on a wire rack and store in an airtight container. They will keep well for 4–5 days.

Or you can try this...

❖ Grated Gruyère, Emmental or a strong mature Cheddar can be substituted for Parmesan.

This spicy tea loaf is made with oil instead of butter. Poppy seeds contain abundant oleic acid (one of the beneficial essential fats) that helps to lower the potentially damaging LDL (low-density lipo-protein) cholesterol, making this a heart-healthy treat.

Seedy courgette nut loaf

3 organic eggs

175g/6oz/scant 1 cup molasses sugar

125ml/4fl oz/½ cup walnut or sunflower oil plus extra for brushing

150g/5oz/1½ cups wholemeal (whole-wheat) flour

150g/5oz/1½ cups plain (all-purpose) flour

1 heaped tsp baking powder

½ tsp bicarbonate of soda (baking soda)

1 tsp ground cinnamon

1 tsp ground ginger

½ tsp allspice

a pinch of salt

2 large or 3 medium courgettes (zucchini), finely grated

50g/2oz/¼ cup Medjool dates, stoned (pitted) and chopped

50g/2oz/scant ½ cup chopped pecans or walnuts

4 tbsp poppy seeds

Makes: 1 large loaf
Prep: 15 minutes
Cook: 1¼ hours

1 Preheat the oven to 180°C, 350°F, gas mark 4. Lightly oil a 900g/2lb loaf tin and line with baking parchment.

2 Beat the eggs, sugar and oil in a food processor until well blended. Sift in the flours, baking powder, bicarbonate of soda (baking soda), spices and salt. Fold in gently on a low speed.

3 Squeeze any excess moisture out of the grated courgettes (zucchini) and mix in gently with the dates, nuts and poppy seeds.

4 Pour the mixture into the prepared tin and level the top. Bake in the preheated oven for 1¼ hours or until the loaf is well risen and golden brown. When it is cooked, a thin skewer inserted into the centre will come out clean.

5 Leave the loaf to cool in the tin for 15 minutes, then turn out onto a wire rack and leave until cold. Wrapped in kitchen foil and stored in an airtight container in a cool place, this will keep well for 2–3 days. It will keep for longer if it is stored in the refrigerator but it tastes best at room temperature. Serve sliced.

Or you can try this...

❖ Add some diced stem ginger in syrup, a handful of raisins or the grated zest of an orange or lemon.

This healthy, high-fibre loaf is quick and easy to make as it doesn't use yeast or require any kneading or rising. It tastes good with cheese, or spread with fruity jam. Linseed has a beneficial omega-3 to omega-6 ratio, helping to reduce inflammatory conditions, such as asthma and rheumatoid arthritis, as well as skin complaints, such as rosacea. This recipe allows the linseeds to swell and supply fibre without irritating the digestive tract lining.

Multi-seed loaf

250g/9oz/2½ cups wholemeal (whole-wheat) flour

100g/3½oz/1 cup rolled oats

50g/2oz ground linseed

a pinch of salt

25g/1oz/scant ¼ cup pumpkin seeds

25g/1oz/scant ¼ cup sunflower seeds

50g/2oz/½ cup linseeds

2 tbsp sesame seeds

1 tsp ground cinnamon

a good pinch of grated nutmeg

150g/5oz/1 cup raisins

50g/2oz/generous ½ cup chopped hazelnuts plus extra for sprinkling

300ml/½ pint/1¼ cups skimmed milk or almond milk

1 tbsp malt extract

2 organic eggs

Makes: 1 large loaf
Prep: 15 minutes
Stand: 20–30 minutes
Cook: 1 hour

1   Preheat the oven to 190°C, 375°F, gas mark 5. Lightly grease or oil a 900g/2lb loaf tin and line with baking parchment.

2   In a large bowl, mix together the flour, oats, ground linseed and salt. Stir in the seeds, spices, raisins and nuts.

3   In another bowl, beat together the milk, malt extract and eggs, and then stir these into the dry ingredients until thoroughly mixed. If the mixture is too stiff add another 1–2 tablespoons milk to loosen it.

4   Leave to stand for 20–30 minutes, then transfer to the prepared tin. Scatter the extra nuts over the top and press in lightly.

5   Bake in the preheated oven for 1 hour or until the loaf is cooked through. When it is cooked, a thin skewer inserted into the centre will come out clean.

6   Cool on a wire rack and serve cut into slices. The loaf will keep well for 3–4 days.

Or you can try this...

❖ For a more savoury flavour, add some caraway or cumin seeds.

❖ Spice it up with some ground or freshly grated ginger, or a good pinch of allspice.

This cake is moist and rich without being heavy, and has a complex spicy flavour. The cardamom seeds are a superb source of calcium and magnesium to support heart health, as well as antioxidants to boost immunity in the gut, and the full range of B vitamins required for energy production.

Seedy moist beetroot cake

180ml/6fl oz/¾ cup extra-virgin olive oil plus extra for greasing

200g/7oz/scant 1 cup light brown sugar

3 organic eggs, separated

225g/8oz/2¼ cups plain (all-purpose) flour, sifted

1 tsp baking powder

½ tsp bicarbonate of soda (baking soda)

a pinch of salt

2 tsp mixed spice

175g/6oz raw beetroot (beets), washed and roughly grated

4 tbsp poppy seeds

3 tbsp sunflower seeds

seeds from 8 green cardamom pods

50g/2oz/generous ¼ cup sultanas (golden raisins)

grated zest and juice of 1 orange

icing (confectioner's) sugar for dusting

crème fraîche and poppy seeds to serve

Serves: 8
Prep: 20 minutes
Cook: 40–45 minutes

1 Preheat the oven to 180°C, 350°F, gas mark 4. Lightly oil a 20cm/8in cake tin and line with baking parchment.

2 Beat the oil and sugar until well mixed. Beat in the egg yolks, one at a time, and then add the flour, baking powder, bicarbonate of soda (baking soda), salt and mixed spice. Beat until thoroughly combined.

3 Add the beetroot (beets), seeds, sultanas (golden raisins), orange zest and juice and mix on a low speed.

4 In a clean, dry bowl, beat the egg whites until stiff, then fold into the cake mixture with a metal spoon in a figure-of-eight motion.

5 Spoon the mixture into the prepared tin, smoothing the top, and bake in the preheated oven for 40–45 minutes or until well risen and a thin skewer inserted into the centre comes out clean.

6 Leave the cake to cool in the tin. Turn out and dust lightly with icing (confectioner's) sugar.

7 Serve cut into slices with a bowl of crème fraîche sprinkled with poppy seeds.

Or you can try this...

❖ For a chocolatey flavour, add 2–3 tablespoons cocoa powder with the flour.

❖ Make the cake spicier by adding a pinch of ground cinnamon and some nutmeg with the mixed spice.

In this contemporary seed cake, the lemon zest and juice add a refreshing citrus flavour while the yoghurt makes the finished cake lighter and moister than the traditional version. The vitamin C of the citrus fruit creates a cake that may help to lower LDL cholesterol, while the seeds' calcium and magnesium improve digestive function.

Poppy seed and lemon cake

175g/6oz/¾ cup butter

175g/6oz/¾ cup golden caster (superfine) sugar

3 organic eggs

250g/9oz/2½ cups self-raising (self-rising) flour, sifted

5 tbsp poppy seeds

grated zest of 2 lemons

juice of 1 lemon

100g/3½oz/½ cup natural Greek yoghurt

lemon zest slivers to decorate

Cream cheese icing (frosting):

125g/4oz/generous ½ cup soft cream cheese

3 tbsp natural Greek yoghurt

2 tbsp icing (confectioner's) sugar

juice of ½ small lemon

Serves: 8–10
Prep: 15 minutes
Cook: 45 minutes

1 Preheat the oven to 180°C, 350°F, gas mark 4. Grease a 20 x 12cm (12 x 8in) deep loaf tin and line with baking parchment.

2 Beat the butter and sugar until light, pale and fluffy. Beat in the eggs, one at a time, beating well between each addition. Add a little of the sifted flour to prevent the mixture from curdling.

3 Add the flour, poppy seeds and lemon zest and mix well on a slow speed. Beat in the lemon juice and Greek yoghurt.

4 Spoon the mixture into the prepared tin and smooth the top. Bake in the preheated oven for about 45 minutes or until well risen and a thin skewer inserted into the centre comes out clean.

5 Leave to cool in the tin for 10 minutes, then turn out onto a wire rack and leave until completely cool.

6 Make the cream cheese icing (frosting): put all the ingredients in a bowl and beat well until thoroughly combined. Spread over the top and decorate with slivers of lemon zest.

Or you can try this...

❖ Instead of using cream cheese, make some lemon icing (frosting) by stirring freshly squeezed lemon juice into some sifted icing (confectioner's) sugar and mixing until you get the desired consistency. Pour over the cake and leave to set.

❖ Pierce the warm cake with a thin skewer while it's still in the tin and pour over some lemon juice sweetened with honey for a sticky, moist version.

This moist and fragrant traybake-style cake made with seasonal fruit makes a great dessert. It's easy to make and needs no decoration. Vanilla seeds are a rich source of the minerals calcium, magnesium and manganese, which together support the regrowth of bone, ligaments, hair and nails.

Greengage and orange cake with vanilla seed cream

175g/6oz/¾ cup butter plus extra for greasing

175g/6oz//¾ cup golden soft brown sugar

3 organic eggs

80g/3oz/generous ½ cup plain (all-purpose) flour

1 tsp baking powder

125g/4oz/1¼ cups ground almonds

grated zest and juice of 1 orange

seeds from 1 vanilla pod (bean)

1–2 tbsp milk

12 ripe greengages, halved and stoned (pitted)

80g/3oz/generous ½ cup whole hazelnuts

Vanilla seed cream:

300ml/½ pint/1¼ cups half-fat crème fraîche

seeds from 1 vanilla pod (bean)

Serves: 8–10
Prep: 20 minutes
Cook: 35–40 minutes

1 Preheat the oven to 180°C, 350°F, gas mark 4. Grease and line a shallow 30 x 20cm (12 x 8in) cake tin with baking parchment.

2 Beat the butter and sugar until soft and fluffy. Add the eggs, one at a time, beating well between each addition. Add a spoonful of flour to help prevent the mixture from curdling.

3 Sift in the rest of the flour and the baking powder and add the ground almonds. Mix on a slow speed until well combined. Add the orange zest and juice, vanilla seeds and a tablespoon or two of milk to slacken the mixture.

4 Spoon the mixture into the prepared cake tin and level the top, pushing the mixture into the corners of the tin.

5 Arrange the greengage halves, cut-side up, in neat lines on top of the cake, then press them down slightly into the mixture. Press the hazelnuts into the cake around them.

6 Bake in the preheated oven for about 35–40 minutes or until the cake rises around the fruit, and a skewer inserted into the centre comes out clean. Leave to cool in the tin.

7 Prepare the vanilla seed cream just before serving. Mix together the crème fraîche and vanilla seeds in a bowl.

8 Serve the cake cut into squares or slices with the vanilla seed cream. Wrapped in kitchen foil, this cake will keep in the refrigerator for 2–3 days. Bring up to room temperature before serving.

Or you can try this...

❖ Substitute apricots, peaches, plums, cherries, blueberries or even raspberries for the greengages.

These delicious little pots are quick and easy to prepare. You can make them the night before for lunch or dinner the following day, but serve at room temperature for maximum flavour. As well as calcium and magnesium, which are needed for regular contraction and relaxation of the heart muscle, cardamom seeds contain potassium, and this helps to balance excess sodium in the body. They also have abundant B vitamins for cellular energy.

Clementine and cardamom chocolate pots

seeds from 10 cardamom pods

300ml/½ pint/1¼ cups double (heavy) cream

200g/7oz plain (semisweet) chocolate (70 per cent cocoa solids)

2 medium egg yolks

25g/1oz/2 tbsp unsalted butter, diced

grated zest and juice of 2 clementines

chocolate shards and candied clementine peel to decorate

Serves: 6
Prep: 10 minutes
Infuse: 20 minutes
Chill: 4 hours

CAUTION! *This recipe contains raw egg yolks, so may not be suitable for pregnant women, infants and people with weakened immune systems.*

1 Slit open the cardamom pods and remove the seeds with a small knife. Alternatively, knock the pods with a rolling pin to release the seeds. Lightly crush the seeds with a pestle and mortar or the back of a spoon.

2 Put the seeds and cream in a small saucepan and heat until the cream is almost boiling. Remove from the heat immediately and set aside to infuse for at least 20 minutes, then strain through a sieve.

3 Break the chocolate into small pieces and place in a bowl suspended over a pan of just simmering water. When the chocolate is melted, remove the bowl from the heat.

4 Whisk the egg yolks until thick and stir them into the melted chocolate with the butter, clementine zest and juice and cream.

5 Divide the mixture between 6 small ceramic pots, ramekins or pretty espresso coffee cups. Cover with cling film (plastic wrap) and chill in the refrigerator for 4 hours or overnight until set.

6 Serve at room temperature decorated with chocolate shards and candied clementine peel.

Or you can try this...

❖ Intensify the flavour by stirring 1 tablespoon orange liqueur into the melted chocolate mixture.

❖ Serve with clementine segments dipped in melted chocolate, then chilled until set, or with some crème fraîche and a sprinkle of clementine zest.

A baked all-American cheesecake is always irresistible and this one is easy to make. It's perfect for a special occasion or when you're entertaining. Vanilla seeds provide bone-building calcium, magnesium and manganese, whilst poppy seeds are rich in oleic acid (an essential fatty acid), which is beneficial for hormone regulation and soft, supple skin.

Baked lemon, vanilla and poppy seed cheesecake

200g/7oz ginger biscuits (cookies), crushed

80g/3oz/scant ½ cup butter, melted

650g/1lb 7oz/scant 3 cups cream cheese or ricotta

200ml/7fl oz/generous ¾ cup sour cream

125g/4oz/½ cup caster (superfine) sugar

1 tbsp cornflour (cornstarch)

4 organic eggs

seeds from 1 vanilla pod (bean)

2 tbsp poppy seeds

grated zest of 2 lemons

juice of 1 lemon

50g/2oz/generous ¼ cup sultanas (golden raisins)

fresh berries to serve, e.g. strawberries, raspberries, redcurrants and white currants

icing (confectioner's) sugar to serve

Serves: 10
Prep: 20 minutes
Chill: 20 minutes
Cook: 45–60 minutes

1 Preheat the oven to 170°C, 325°F, gas mark 3.

2 Mix the crushed biscuits into the melted butter and press onto the base of a 23cm/9in loose-bottomed tart tin (spring-form tart pan). Leave to chill in the refrigerator for 20 minutes.

3 Put the cream cheese or ricotta, sour cream, sugar, cornflour (cornstarch) and eggs in a large bowl or food mixer and beat together.

4 Add the vanilla seeds to the cheese mixture with the poppy seeds, lemon zest and juice, and sultanas (golden raisins). Fold in gently.

5 Remove the tin from the refrigerator and spoon the mixture over the biscuit base. Smooth the top with a palette knife.

6 Cook in the preheated oven for about 1 hour, checking the cheesecake after 45–50 minutes. Remove when it's golden brown on top and springs back when pressed gently.

7 Set aside to cool. Dust lightly with icing (confectioner's) sugar and serve cut into slices with fresh berry fruits.

Or you can try this...

❖ Add some poppy seeds to the crushed biscuits for the base.

❖ For a more lemony flavour, lightly swirl some lemon curd through the cheese mixture before baking.

Index

VICKI EDGSON was a practising nutritional therapist for over 20 years. She has written and co-written 10 titles on nutrition/health and fitness, and contributed to many leading magazines and online forums including *Harper's Bazaar*, *Tatler*, *Red*, *Elle*, *Women's Health*, *Healthy*, *Cosmopolitan* and *Psychologies*. She co-founded The Food Doctor business and has worked with health-food companies including Honestly Healthy, Abel & Cole and Bounce Foods. She has appeared on television in *Fat Nation* for the BBC and *Diet Doctors* for Channel Five, and contributed to the BBC's *Breakfast Show* and ITV's *Lorraine*.

HEATHER THOMAS has been eating and enjoying seeds and plant proteins since she shared a house with five vegetarian Quakers at university and learnt to cook. A food writer and editor, she has written best-selling cookery books including *The New Vegetarian Cookbook* with the Vegetarian Society and *Broth* (co-author Vicki Edgson), and has worked with many top chefs, slimming companies and women's health organizations, as well as contributing to health and food magazines in the UK and the United States.

Acknowledgements:
To Charlotte Stapleton for her superb support in researching the health benefits and history of the seeds we have included, and Nick Barnard of Rude Health for pointing out the real meaning of a pseudograin/cereal – where would we be without our learned colleagues? And, most of all, to my co-author, Heather Thomas, to whom I dedicate this book, as she was able to sort out the wood from the trees when I could not! Vicki Edgson

Assistant food stylist: Charlotte O'Connell. Props: Alexander Breeze